Finding More

PEBBLES ON THE SHORE

MEMORIES OF AN AMERICAN
GROWING UP IN INDIA

Fran Schillinger

Foreword

I have written some eighty stories since my book was published by Amazon in 2011. I considered integrating these new stories into the original book, *Pebbles On The Shore*, but decided to make this a separate book. At this point, my memories have run out. I probably will not be writing any more stories.

These two books have given me the opportunity to share the memories of my life with friends and family. I feel so lucky to have such a unique and special life.

Acknowledgments

I have macular degeneration so I want to thank my dear friend, Dolores Bigger, for her help with translating my illegible writing to the typed page.

I also want to thank my brother-in-law, Bill Kretler, and his daughter, Katie, for their computer expertise in putting this book together.

And then, last but not least, I want to thank my family and friends for sharing my life. Without all these memories this book would not be possible.

Contents

Memories

I stand quietly on the shore. The gentle waves of time
      wash over the pebbles at my feet.
    They tumble and roll with each passing wave.

Pebbles are my memories:
      Some are small and dull
          not worth much time;
      Some are shiny and smooth,
          bringing comfort and peace;
      Others sparkle and flash
          with joy and delight;
      A few are dark and heavy;
          not a place to linger on.

The waves of time have worn away
      the sharp edges of emotions.
These smooth, rounded pebbles of my memory
      are there to be touched and sorted;
To find and remember the sweet treasures of my past...

—Fran Schillinger, 2011

— Years 1 to 20 —

TEACHERS TO REMEMBER

Many decades have passed since my days of being a student and most of my classroom experiences have faded from my memory. However, there are two teachers who have managed to remain vivid in my mind. Both teachers happened to teach laboratory science courses.

The first one was my high school biology class. Mr. Fleming was not the ordinary run of teacher. He had a passion for nature and through his enthusiast and unique approach, was able to transfer his passion on to his students.

Our school was situated in the foothills of the Himalaya Mountains, a locale abundant with temperate zone flora and fauna. One class assignment was to find an extremely rare "Mouseear fern" which only appeared during the four month monsoon rains. I remember my delight, after days of searching, on finding a small hidden clump nestled against a mossy bank. Then there was the dissection of small frogs. Not a favorite of the more squeamish girls. We sent small electric charges into the dead frogs to stimulate kicks and jerks through their legs.

But one demonstration turned out to be a bit too much for even the most scientific of us. Our class met the first period after lunch. We trailed into the classroom to be met by a horrific odor. There, spread out on the demo table at the front of the room, was the complete digestive system of a cow: esophagus, stomach, intestines and all! Our innovative teacher had brought this ghastly mess from a slaughter house. I don't know whether such things normally smell bad when freshly killed but this mess sent us all, choking and gagging, from the room. Being one who joined the mass exit, I don't know how successfully the planned demonstration turned out.

The other laboratory class I vividly remember was my sophomore college physiology class. Mr. Williams had a unique and personalized approach to teaching the subject. At the beginning of the semester each student was made responsible for a young white rat, kept in an individual cage in the lab. Our assignment was to set aside a small portion of everything we ate, including candy, cokes etc. This was to be the exclusive diet for our rat. Over the span of several weeks our rats gave us an indication of whether our diet was healthy or not. Some of the rats developed spasms and hair loss, some even died. The lesson learned was a powerful one. I have never forgotten the importance of a well balanced nutritious diet!

Another assignment was to collect our urine in a jug over a period of three days. (We did take a lot of ribbing over our ever-present jugs from other students). We then analyzed our urine for the state of our health, etc. another vivid revelation.

Then there was the day we studied our own blood under the microscope. It was fascinating to see the red and white corpuscles of your very own blood. In my case, it was apparent something was unusual, unlike the other's slides, there were small dark blobs attached to several of the red corpuscles. When the teacher saw this he became excited and asked me if I had lived in the tropics. When I said I had, he told me the dark blobs were malaria parasites attacking my blood. He was delighted to have diagnosed the condition. He said the last time he had seen that was in graduate school some twenty years ago. As for me, I had been suffering with occasional mild bouts of malaria. However, within three or four years they no longer persisted.

Both Mr. Fleming and Mr. Williams made a lasting impression on my life. Later on, as a teacher myself, I attempted to make my classes relevant to my students and their lives. We all find value in knowledge that we can use in a personal way. Perhaps my love of nature and science can be traced back to those two classes I attended so long ago.

ONE SIZE FITS ALL

Dental care has come a long way since my parent's generation. This is due to regular check-ups and the use of crowns, caps and dental implants. Even at our age few of us have full sets of dentures. This was not so for my parents. As far back as l can remember, they both had complete sets of false teeth. As a young child I can recall thinking they had it easy by being able to clean their teeth just by dropping them into two separate glasses of Polident, no tedious chore of brushing, as I had to do.

There is a family story about dad's false teeth that he had to share with us. This incident took place while he was still a missionary in India. He was the much respected minister of the church in town. He had gone down to the train depot to meet a passenger arriving on an incoming train. As he stood waiting on the unpaved platform, he had the urge to sneeze! Much to his embarrassment, his upper denture flew out of his mouth and landed before him in the dirt. He looked around, hoping no one had noticed, and carefully wiped the dirt from the teeth as best he could. Having just placed the denture back in his mouth, he was horrified to see one of his church deacons approaching him, carefully carrying a bowl of water for him to wash his teeth. There was nothing to do except take the wayward denture back out of his mouth and rinse it off in the water with a feeling of total chagrin! He did so as he mumbled expressions of gratitude and embarrassed apologies. Neither man ever referred to the incident again, though I'm sure it was told to others in the congregation to their amusement.

There is another family story that I can remember having to do with my parent's dentures. This happened after their retirement from being missionaries in India. They were visiting with my brother, John, and his wife, Miriam, who were living in St. Louis. One morning Mother got up before dad, dressed and came downstairs to join John and Miriam for breakfast. As they were eating the meal and visiting, dad rushed into the kitchen with great indignation. In his hand he carried a set of false teeth and sputtered through toothless gums, "Helen, you are wearing my teeth!" After the laughter died down, the teeth were returned to the rightful owners, and all was forgiven. But I can't help but wonder if the mix up had even happened before without their being aware of the mistake. After all, it appears that one size fits all!

GRANDMA'S GRAPE ARBOR

Our family was on furlough from the missionary field in India. We were living with my grandmother in Coraopolis, PA, a suburb of Pittsburgh. The back yard joined with the neighbor's yards without any fences for almost the entire block. This was a perfect place for the neighborhood children to play.

I was ten years old and my brother, Stan, was twelve. We were just the right age to join in play with all the kids in the neighborhood. On long summer evenings after supper we would all organize games of softball, touch football, hide and seek, kick the can, and many more I have forgotten. We would play until night fell and our folks called us in to go to bed. What a wonderful time we had.

My grandmother had a fine grape arbor. After many years of loving care, the vines had grown to make a lovely bower where one could sit and enjoy the cool shade. They were concord grapes. The same grapes used in the famous Welch's brand. When ripe, the procedure was to squeeze the skin to pop the sweet juice surrounding the seeds into your mouth. It was best not to chew the inner pulp that held the seeds as it was were quite sour. One just swallowed it whole much like how one eats raw oysters. Actually, I haven't had a concord grape for many years; they don't seem to be available in our markets.

One of those summer evenings as we were deciding on which game we would play, someone spotted grandma's grape arbor. The grapes were fully ripe, plump and juicy. After sampling a few, somehow the war started. Soon all the kids were grabbing handfuls of grapes to throw at each other. It was a free-for-all. Grapes flew everywhere, squashed on the grass, sprayed on the white houses, and smashed on clothes and hair. The juicy fruit was everywhere! Of course, all of this was without grandma's knowledge. The next morning Stan and I, with a few subdued friends, had to clean up the mess we had made and a zero harvest for grapes that year!

I look at the way children play today. I do hope that in the small towns throughout our country children still play those games we did as children. It was such a wonderful opportunity for imagination, self imposed rules, sportsmanship and so many other ways to relate to one's peers. It seems that today with all the adult oriented sports and crowded schedules, the children do not have any time to play together without adult supervision. I know part of it is the fear of an abduction, thanks to our panic oriented media. But I do feel sad that our young children of today don't have those opportunities to play as we used to play.

I do still feel a little remorse over grandma's grapes, but I guess that was part of growing up and besides, it was a lot of fun!

A STOCKING STORY

Fashions come and go, often to repeat the styles, otherwise how would the fashion industry survive? I have discovered that if one holds onto one's clothes long enough, the fashion will come around again; a real money saver!

But here l would like to discuss the matter of leg coverings. Probably with the invention of shoes, people discovered they needed a layer next to the foot to prevent blisters, so stockings were invented. Somewhere along the line the term "hosiery" was used to imply a little more refinement.

As a teenager living in the 1940's, I lived through a dramatic evolution of hosiery. Our mothers had hosiery make of silk. Very delicate and fragile, prone to runs, so that they lasted for only a few wearings. My generation was introduced to "rayon" hosiery. Not too great; rayon was inclined to get baggy and pooch out at the knees after sitting. Also it was very important to be sure the seam was straight up the back of the leg. These stockings were held up by "garter belts", a miserable contraption of elastic bands and garters. Or one could wear a girdle to squash in all the tummy bumps, with garters attached, to hold up the stockings.

However, when the war started it was almost impossible to find stockings. As a result "leg makeup" was the only thing available to look like stockings. Now this was really miserable stuff. After smearing it all up and down your legs it looked ok for a short while but it was inclined to rub off on anything it touched, especially if you were perspiring, including furniture, clothing and bedding! When l think of leg makeup one incident comes to mind. At our high school graduation we were all dressed up in our finest outfits. With no stockings available we all smeared on leg makeup. As we gathered together for the ceremony we collapsed into laughter to see one of our classmates, who having never previously worn leg makeup, had failed to shave her legs. Each hair stood out, coated with makeup. Her legs looked like they were covered with beige fur. Poor gal was mortified. We all managed to help her clean off the makeup so her legs were more normal in appearance.

Of course in the years since then, hosiery has come a long way. With the development of nylon stockings made into pantyhose most of our problems of the past are solved. But l do hope the present generation of women can appreciate what the women of the past suffered through to stay in fashion.

SMALLPOX—
THE SCOURGE OF MANKIND

Smallpox has been one of the diseases that have plagued humans for centuries. It is usually fatal, especially for those without any immunity to the disease, but if one should survive they were left scarred for life with deep pits on face and the rest of the body. When the Europeans first came to America they brought smallpox with them. The native population had no immunity to the disease so, along with other diseases and warfare, the result was the loss of 90% of the native population.

As a child of American missionaries growing up in India had its hazards. From infancy we were required to get a smallpox vaccination every two years in order for us to not contract the virus. I remember two family stories that made us thankful for those vaccinations. There was a tradition for an annual Sunday school picnic to be held during the early spring before the weather became too hot. As the minister, Dad would make arrangements with the railroad to drop us, some hundred people, off at a river bank closest to the railroad tracks. It was a lovely sandy beach where we could play games and swim in the river. All the mothers brought enough food to feed an army. We played games and spent the day swimming in the cool water. One year, after a full day of fun, we were waiting for the train to come by to take us home. A few of us wandered upstream along the riverbank. Just up around a bend in the river we discovered a naked corpse of a man who was covered with smallpox sores. It is Hindu tradition to burn their dead but, with the chance of contracting a dreaded disease, in this case they had just thrown the body in the river. It was caught up in some riverside weeds just a couple hundred yards above where we had been swimming all day. Needless to say, we all received additional vaccinations just to be sure we were safe.

The other story has to do with the time our mother was traveling on a crowded train. It was late evening when she got on the train. The third class compartment had rows of benches running the length of the compartment. There was a dim light at the end of the room. During the night a woman sitting fairly close to mother was having trouble quieting a fussy baby in her arms. She seemed to be exhausted and mother offered to take the baby for a while. However, the baby kept on with fitful sleep. As dawn came, mother looked more closely at the baby in her arms to discover the infant was covered with smallpox sores. She handed the baby back to the mother and got off the train at the next stop to find the health administrator to get a booster vaccination. She was grateful to have not contracted the disease.

Thankfully now smallpox is no longer present, due to a worldwide vaccination program of eradication. But for many centuries it was one of the scourges of mankind, as I can attest to first hand.

PEARL HARBOR—
THAT DAY OF INFAMY

As we remember that day on December 7th seventy years ago, it reminds me of how much that day changed my life. It was 1941 and I was thirteen years old. I, and my brother Stan, were home on vacation from boarding school. On that Sunday afternoon we heard a bulletin broadcast over the radio with the voice of President Roosevelt making his famous speech about the surprise bombing of Pearl Harbor and the declaration of war. I was surprised to see both dad and mother with tears in their eyes when they heard the news. Of course for them, having lived through the First World War, they knew what pain and sorrow was to come. Little did I realize how my world was about to change!

Our town was located in the Province of Bengal, in the far eastern part of India. The Japanese had swept through southern Asia and the islands of the Pacific, almost without resistance. They were successful in the invasion of Burma; the next door neighbor to India. There was a real concern that they would next make an assault into India where we lived.

At this time India was ruled by the British, so there was already a strong British army presence in our area. But within a year after Pearl Harbor the American armed forces began to flood the region. First came the army engineers to build the army barracks and airfield runways. Next came the mass of mighty equipment and personnel of the air force. By the winter of 1943 there were some fifty thousand American troops in five air bases within fifty miles of our town of Khargur.

From these bases bombing raids were run into Burma and China, even "over the hump" (so called as the bombers had to fly up over the eastern section of the Himalaya's which towered 28,000 to 32,000 feet high).

I went away to boarding school in north India for nine months of the year, but when I returned home in December through March of my high school years l was immersed in a flood of American soldiers. They were everywhere; driving Jeeps and command cars on the streets and bazaars, attending my dad's church services and our social gatherings.

For a typical young teenage girl, this was about as good as it gets as l was one of only two American girls in the whole region. Looking back on that experience I'm sure most of those young men thought of me more as a kid sister, but I must say all that attention was great fun! Of course, I did fall in love several times, though most of my dates were under the watchful eyes of my parents. However, as it turned out, one of those infatuations turned later into real love. After attending college in America, I married one of those handsome soldiers I had met in India.

All of that huge build up of armed strength must have paid off. The Japanese only tried one three-plane bombing run into India and never tried to invade. I left India in the summer of 1945 to attend college in Pennsylvania. I was amazed and bemused to discover that in the college I attended (Indiana State Teacher's College of Indiana, PA) in the student body of two thousand there were only two men! The men were still off fighting a war. The girls on campus were starved for contact with men, what a wild contrast to my recent experience! By the next school year the war was over, the men all returned and the male/female ratio returned to normal.

LIFE IN THE HIMALAYAS

My parents were missionaries in India. There were many other missionaries there from various denominations. The tropical heat of the Indian lowlands is quite uncomfortable for westerners from more moderate climates. The various missions got together to establish a school for their children in the Himalayan Mountains. The school was situated in the "foothills" at an elevation of seven thousand feet. Stretching off to the North was range after range with elevations of twenty to thirty thousand feet.

It was a boarding school of about four hundred students. The school year was from March to November with vacation time during the cooler winter months when the children would return to their homes in the lowlands. When the children were younger the mothers would rent one of the numerous cottages surrounding the school to provide a home environment for the young ones. The dads would spend their six week vacations with the family during the most severe summer months. As children we all loved boarding school where you could be with your friends twenty-four hours a day. But it was also great fun to live off school grounds with your parents and siblings.

The mountain scenery was lovely. The hillsides were covered by forests of long needled pines, massive moss covered oak trees, and meadows of wild dahlias in every color, as well as other flowers. There were no cars or paved roads. Most of the paths were narrow trails following the contours of the mountain. The only means of transportation were coolie driven devices. And for small children, a kundi, a basket with a seat carried on a coolie's back. For adults, a single enclosed chair suspended from shoulder poles carried by two men in front and two to the rear. This was called a "dandy". For the one road wide enough, one could also hire a rickshaw, which could carry two people. This ran on two wheels with two men pulling from the front and two men pushing from the rear. It was usually a thrilling ride as the rickshaw drivers loved to run at full speed along the twisting mountain road, missing the edge by mere inches.

As children growing up in those mountains we were almost like mountain goats. We were so used to scrambling up the mountain paths we thought nothing of climbing a thousand feet from our high school dormitory building to the school for classes. After school hours and weekends we were free to roam over the hillside exploring and playing made-up games. One of our favorite activities was to gather the abundant pine needles into a high pile below a ledge or big tree where we could jump into the soft pile time after time. Of course, we also played the usual games of children; hide and seek, kick the can and capture the flag.

During the months of the monsoon rains the mountains were transformed. From June through August the rain swept up over the lowlands to bring relief to a parched earth. As the rain clouds bumped into the Himalayans it came down in torrents, even an umbrella could not keep you dry. Every oak tree sprouted ferns on trunk and branches; the forests were filled with ferns and wild orchids grew in the meadows. The air was washed clean of haze and dust. On clear nights the stars were so bright and looked close enough to touch. It didn't rain every day of course; on clear days we delighted in finding mountain streams to splash and play in the crystal pools and waterfalls.

The school was just the perfect size, large enough to have thirty or so students for every grade level, but not so large as to prevent even those with limited skills having a chance to participate. Through the years our close friendships were a bond that held us together. Even to this day I feel that loving bond.

OLD CRAFTY POISON IVY

When going for walks in the woods we have all been warned to watch out for poison ivy or poison oak. Not only should you not touch it, but also one should be careful not to let it brush against your clothes. However, if you happen to have a rambunctious dog along, it is another problem as we found out the hard way.

We all blossomed out with rashes from touching our pooch after returning from a hike in the forest. My dad told me of a time when he was fooled. As a boy growing up on a farm in eastern Pennsylvania, he had lots of run-ins with poison ivy. He became quite famous among the children in the area for he was the only child immune to poison ivy. He delighted in showing off by rubbing it on his skin with no effect. When he went off to college for four years, his siblings perpetuated the story of his immunity. So one summer on his return home, a whole crowd of children gathered to witness this miracle. He obligingly rolled around in a large patch of the stuff. But alas, somehow he had lost his immunity and was completely covered from head to toe with a severe itchy rash, much to the delight of the other children. He stayed clear of the plant from then on.

My husband told another story about poison oak to me. When he was a teenager a bunch of boys was making a fire. It was winter in California and they wanted to keep warm. All the leaves had fallen so as they gathered up brush from the surrounding woods they couldn't tell what they had collected. They got a roaring blaze going and enjoyed the fire's warmth. As with all campfires there was quite a lot of smoke. They soon became aware of their eyes and noses becoming irritated. Some of the twigs they had used were poison oak. They all developed a very severe reaction. Not only were their eyes swollen shut, but they also had serious respiratory reactions and had to spend a few days in bed.

As a child growing up in the mountains in India, there was a different plant to watch out for called stinging nettle. It grew one to three feet tall and the stems and leaves were covered by tiny hairs that were full of toxin. Just a casual brush against your skin would make you instantly develop an itchy, painful rash. It seemed to grow everywhere; we were forever running into the stuff.

However, we discovered that where stinging nettle grew, we could always find the antidote; it was called dock leaf. A small plant that grew close to the ground with a large smooth leaf. If one could grab a leaf or two and rub it over the stinging nettle rash, it would instantly relieve the discomfort. We were grateful to Mother Nature for being so helpful. I haven't heard of such an antidote for poison ivy and oak. It seems that Mother Nature does have a few tricks up her sleeve for the unsuspecting traveler in the forest.

THE OL' SWIMMING HOLE

To be fair, l have to admit we did have a swimming pool at our boarding school. But it was not much to brag about. It was located at the older boys hostel inside an annex to the main building. Olympic sized, but uncirculated and unheated. With the school located at an elevation of seven thousand feet, I have a vivid memory of that pool always at a temperature barely above freezing. The boys were expected to use the pool several times a week as part of their routine. However it was not one of the favorite activities, especially as they didn't bother with swimsuits.

The high school girls, who lived in another dormitory across the valley, were allowed to use the pool only on Saturday afternoons. We were encouraged, but not required, to participate. However, there was one rather small enticement to go swimming. The boys' restrooms were located adjacent to the swimming pool. Through the years, by some mysterious means, peek holes had developed in the wall overlooking the pool. Of course, we girls, unlike the boys, wore swimsuits. But we did enjoy the knowledge that our every move was probably being observed by eyeballs pressed to those peepholes. It almost made up for the freezing water temperature. However, one day we girls almost turned the tables on the boys. It seems that the communications got mixed up. One Saturday afternoon when we arrived at the pool, the boys didn't know we were coming. As we opened the outside door to the pool and walked in we discovered numerous boys there in the buff! There was a lot of yelling and wild dashing for the exit door to their restroom. I remember mostly little white rear ends in mad retreat. It was fun to later tease them about what we saw.

It was a tradition to have an annual swimming competition. This always took place during the warmest time of the year. Bleachers were set up around the entire pool, enough to seat one to two hundred people. It was a lot of fun to compete against other grade levels. In diving, relays and even water polo games, of course, the boys wore swimsuits for that event. One incident stands out in my memory. One of the competitions was for underwater swimming endurance. The contest was to swim as many laps as possible without coming to the surface to breathe. On this day, several of the older boys were competing. They dropped out, one by one, until only one boy was left swimming alone at the bottom of the large pool. The crowd was quite in awe of how long he was able to hold his breath. However, he did seem to be slowing down. He was still moving his arms and legs, but not very purposefully. It was then, as if in unison, everyone watching seemed to realize the boy was actually unconscious. Several boys dove in to pull him out of the pool. Indeed, he was unconscious and almost dead. The coach administered CPR, the water gushed out of his lungs and his life was saved. However, that was the last time underwater endurance was included in the competition.

As l think back to that old swimming pool, I am amazed that we even had the fortitude to get into that ice bath. But then, it seems kids will do almost anything, as long as it means doing it together.

THE SCHOOL TRAIN

For us kids probably one of the best experiences of boarding school was the train trip to get there. Woodstock School was located in the foothills of the Himalayas in north central India. The students, numbering about 450, came from all parts of the Indian sub-continent and even as far away as Burma and Singapore. In the 1930's and 40's the roads were unpaved and congested; the only prudent way to travel was by train. The school year ran from March through November in order to provide an alternative to the intense summer heat of the lower elevations. This meant that twice a year we got to join the "school party" organized to take us to school. For the children of our mission, which was located in Bengal, this meant boarding the train in early evening, traveling all the next day and night in order to cover the thousand plus miles to our school? Every March our parents would bring us from our homes in that part of the country to the Calcutta train depot. For us kids this was when the fun began. After all, we hadn't seen each other for over three months (a long time from a child's perspective). Generally our group consisted of 12 to 15 children and a very brave chaperon (usually a teacher, or reluctant parent). I use the word "brave" because to keep the lid on a bunch of boisterous children ranging in age from 6 to 17 for over 36 hours is quite a challenge!

Let me take a moment to explain the set up on the train. Unlike American trains, each coach was separate with no corridor through to adjoining coaches. First and Second class were separate compartments with access only from the outside door. The Third class of compartments took up the entire railroad coach with one access door. A back-to-back row of wooden benches ran down the center of the compartment. Below the windows on each side, a continuous bench faced inwards. Then above these benches were upper berths to hold luggage and odds and ends. The bathroom had a small basin to wash hands. The toilet was a hole in the floor with two six inch high pedestals for your feet on each side of the hole which opened to the track under the train where you could seen the ground rushing by below.

In order to keep us all together we always traveled in third class. We each had a bedroll which was designed to open out into a bed sized pad with blankets and had a large pocket at each end to hold small items and serve as a pillow. In addition, we all had a small trunk for clothes, etc. At nighttime we rolled out our bedrolls end to end on the hard wooden benches and slept in our clothes. It would be some time before we all finally settled down to sleep. We could hardly wait for the arrival of the next day.

As the train had no dining car, it was left up to the passengers to buy their food from vendors who hawked their food on the station platforms. As children growing up in India, we had been trained to buy only food that was freshly cooked. Nothing raw or cold from street vendors. With a few coins in hand we delighted in checking out the available foods. One treat was hot tea made the Indian way with lots of milk and sugar. The tea "walla" carried a large silver jug on his head as he called out "Gorrham Chai" to advertise his "hot tea". With no disposable cups available, the tea was served in small clay cups to be smashed after use. Just to be a part of the "true India" with all its noisy crowds, bustle, sights, sounds and smells was great fun. But our favorite stop of all was Lucknow station. It was there that the whole depot was overrun with Rhesus monkeys. They were everywhere: on top of the train, mingling among the people and on the platform looking for a chance to grab any available food item. They even came boldly through the open windows of the train to snatch goodies from unsuspecting travelers. We loved to watch their antics and bold behavior. At the blast of the train whistle announcing departure, the monkeys would make a hasty retreat to wait for the arrival of the next train.

Between stations, as we rumbled through the countryside, we spent hours hanging our heads out of the open windows letting the wind blow in our faces and waving at farmers working the land. Our modem trains with their sealed windows are not nearly as much fun!

After spending a second night on the train we awoke early to find we were approaching the first range of mountains. This area was less populated and contained the beginning of the mountain forests. In the early light we could hear and see wild peacocks perched on branches. We would soon be arriving at Derha Doon, the end of our train journey. But this would not be our final destination. The train ride brought us to an elevation of two thousand feet; we still had five thousand feet yet to go. We were, along with our luggage, loaded onto a bus to travel on a one-way steep, twisting road up the mountain. After climbing another four thousand feet, we disembarked at Kingkraig, the end of the paved road. From there it was necessary to walk, or for the little children, ride in a basket on a porter's back for an additional five miles, and up another thousand feet, to the school. There we could greet all of our other classmates and friends. Another school year would begin, with all the expectations of what that would bring. But the journey to get there was already a great part of the fun!

GREEK "REFUGEES"

It was the summer of 1945; the war in Europe was finally over. After months of waiting, I had been able to obtain passage on a ship from India to New York. The ship was the Gripshoim, a Swedish ocean liner. Our route was from Bombay, India, through the Suez Canal into the Mediterranean and across the Atlantic to New York. The passengers on board were a mixed lot. Many were missionaries, an assortment of stranded travelers and a large contingent of multi-national soldiers. An interesting mix, to say the least.

As we emerged into the Mediterranean from the Suez Canal we were told by the ship's staff that we were going to make an unscheduled stop in Athens, Greece. It seemed that at the outbreak of war in Europe there were a number of American citizens of Greek decent who were visiting in Greece and had become trapped there for the duration of the war. Now that peace had been restored they were finally able to return to the states. The ship's personnel, and many of the passengers on board, assumed these poor refugees had endured great hardships and would be in need of many of the necessities of life, such as clothing, etc. due to all the years of war and privation. With the good missionaries in the lead, all the passengers were asked to donate whatever they could spare to help out these most unfortunate refugees. By the time we anchored in the harbor of Athens, there were rows of tables lined up on the deck with piles and piles of donated clothing and other essentials. As the launches from the port began to arrive loaded with the refugees, we all hung over the ship's rails to watch them come aboard. It was immediately obvious we had made an erroneous assumption. Not only did these refugees have copious amounts of luggage, but in addition, carried armload's of fur coats and other expensive items. It seemed they were certainly not in need of our help. There was a mad scramble to get the tables of donated clothing out of sight as we did not wish to offend them.

As the voyage continued on to New York, we shared the joy and delight of our new passengers. They were so happy to be returning to American they infected the whole ship. Every night, to the accompaniment of accordion music played by one of the group, on deck they danced wonderful Greek dances well into the night. Some of us were caught up in the festivities and found ourselves joining in with the dancing. I do remember l was quite interested in the fact that they all seemed to smell of olive oil. Just as a side note, it does seem that various ethnic societies throughout the world do have they very own odor. Probably the result of diet and personal grooming.

The remainder of the voyage was made more interesting by the addition of those delightful "poor" refugees. Another experience to be remembered fondly.

A SHIP OF FANTASY

There were three fruit trees that grew in our large backyard in India. A very old and luxurious mango tree dominated an area at the rear of the compound. The mangos were hardly worth the effort to harvest them because they had a strong acid flavor and were full of stringy pulp. Dad decided it was not worth the water cost and had it removed. Right outside the back door grew a bale tree. I have never met anyone who has ever heard of that variety of fruit tree. But it was sort of fun; it grew grapefruit sized, hard shelled fruit. When the shell turned from green to yellow one could use a pole to dislodge the fruit. In order to break the shell it took several hard slams on the floor. The next step was to scoop out the stringy orange pulp. This was pressed in a sieve to extract the flavorful concentrated juice. It tasted like a cross between a peach and an apricot. We diluted the pulp with water and added a little sugar. I had fun going through all the required steps to enjoy the final result.

The third fruit tree was a huge cashew nut tree. For anyone who has never seen one, it is quite interesting. The thin shelled cashews protrude from the end of a small yellow inedible fruit. When the fruit withers, the nut is ready to harvest. It is this cashew tree that brings back so many fond memories. At the age of seven or eight, while I was away at boarding school, a powerful monsoon storm blew the cashew tree down. On our return home for our three month vacation, it was stretched out on the ground, intact; a root ball, huge trunk and bare branches sticking high into the air. Probably dad had left it there to dry out before cutting it up into firewood. But for me, my brother, Stan, and our gang of friends it became a ship to provide the fantasy of wonderful adventure. The large root ball became the stern, where the "Captain" could perch among the roots to steer the ship off to any destination desired. The trunk was broad enough to traverse with ease, and the sturdy branches made wonderful perches to serve as the crow's nest where the lookout could watch for enemy ships, or any other imagined danger, such as giant whales, etc. We spent many hours playing on our wonderful ship of imagination that vacation time. What a delight it was, as children, to play those games of make believe. We learned so many lessons of cooperation, making and following self imposed rules, inventing our own games of fun, and most important, developing our imagination and creativity. My wish is for every child to be left alone, with unstructured time, long enough to discover that wonderful world of fantasy and make believe.

A HALLOWEEN PRANK

It was my senior year in high school. I guess we got the idea when we discovered that the skylight window in the chemistry lab was never locked. With a little more investigation, we also discovered it was possible to get onto the chemistry lab roof by jumping onto it from an adjacent hillside. So that was how our plan for Halloween mischief evolved. On the night of Halloween, after making sure the coast was clear, I and four of my classmates met to carry out our plan. With flashlights in hand we lowered ourselves from the skylight onto the tables below. From there we were able to gain access to the other classrooms on the same floor. Our high school was made up of some one hundred and fifty students, so each of the four grade levels had between thirty to forty students. Each grade level had a "home room" where students stored their books, notebooks, etc. in one of those old fashioned desks with a compartment under the desktop. Our plan was to move every desk to another room in random order but making sure they were left in perfect rows, so as not to raise any suspicions. It took us more than two hours to accomplish our task. The next morning, as the students went to their "home rooms" for the first period of the day, pandemonium broke loose. Not only did they find their desks were out of order, but not even in the same room. To our delight, it took more than two hours of school time to finally work out the mess and reposition the lost desks. Of course we the perpetrators acted just as confused as everyone else, while inwardly chuckling over the success of our prank.

Even though there was much speculation over who could have done such a disruptive thing, and with teachers trying to determine whom the culprits were, we were never discovered. I am sure that by now, the statute of time limitations has long passed. We couldn't be given our just punishment. But I will always remember that Halloween prank with gleeful satisfaction. For after all, it was just clean fun, and we were never caught!

MY AYAH

For the average person raised in the USA, it is difficult to understand the bond that develops between a small child and her caretaker. Perhaps the closed parallel would be a live-in grandmother who has taken over the full time help of childcare. However, as a child born in India, it was a necessary fact of life. As a missionary, my mother had many responsibilities, which required time away from daily household chores. Facilities were quite primitive and inconvenient such as a coal burning stove, no running water, and very minimal refrigeration. To hire help was the answer. At very low cost my parents hired five employees from the native population. She hired my ayah (nursemaid) and her husband as our cook, an assistant to help the cook and serve meals, a man to clean the very large two-story bungalow and a gardener. The total expense of having these servants was less than one hundred dollars a month. They were also provided living accommodations on the property. For that time, in the mid nineteen hundreds, was a good wage. The cook, Abhoy, and ayah were able to support their three children through a college education.

Of course, in my memories, my ayah was just a part of my baby world. She was there when I woke each morning. She was with me-through the morning. After lunch, when it was naptime, she would go home for a couple of hours then return to help me with my daily bath, playtime and dinner (served earlier than my parents dinner) then helping with bedtime. Her final responsibility of the day was to sit by my bed until I fell asleep when she could finally go home. I remember, on a couple of occasions, being a typical bratty kid, pretending to fall asleep, waiting for her to leave, and then making a big fuss until she came back to stay with me longer. I presume my parents put a stop to that particular stunt!

In my memory, ayah was a gentle, sweet woman. She was soft and warm and loved to hold me in her arms. She always wore a white sari and smelled fresh and clean with a hint of sandalwood and coconut oil. She spoke no English, but her own village dialect called "Areha". In fact, I learned to speak her dialect and English simultaneously. The first sentence I ever spoke was a poem she taught me in Areha: "ay, ay chandi" which translates to "come, come moon". "

With all her sweet and gentle ways, there was one thing I learned to dread. At bath time, when she would dry me with a big, soft towel, she insisted it was important to pull each of my fingers until the knuckle joint popped! This was, she told me, to prevent arthritis later on. (It didn't work! I got arthritis anyway!)

I had the joy of her love and attention until I started boarding school. When I was seven years old ayah and her husband, our cook, retired and moved back to their village some distance away. I only saw my ayah one more time. I was in my early teens; we made a trip to see our cook and ayah in their village. It was not a happy experience. I was so thrilled to see my dear ayah again, but as we hugged and cried I was horrified to discover I had lost my ability to understand or speak her language! I had not heard, or spoken her dialect since she had left. We laughed and hugged and I pretended to understand her words. But my heart was breaking. It was so very sad to lose my connection with this precious woman who had been such an important part of my early childhood. How fortunate I was to have had her in my life.

MISSION HOTEL

In 1922 my parents became missionaries with the North American Baptist Mission Society. They were sent to serve in the provinces of Bengal/Orissa mission fields in India. As they were in their 30's, they were deemed too old to attend language school for two years. The mission field consisted of several outposts in villages or small towns where ten to twelve missionary families were placed. They ran schools, medical clinics and organized Christian churches. There was only one position that didn't require knowledge of the native languages; this was where my parents were assigned.

The town of Kharapur was a railroad center developed by the British who had established an extensive railroad system throughout India. The town had a population of some 60,000, a mixture of British hierarchy, Anglo-Indians (a mixed race from British-Indian relations) and Indians. The British mostly attended the Anglican Church in town. However, the Baptist mission had built a church to serve the Anglo-Indian population, all of who spoke English and lived a European lifestyle. My father served as Minister of the church, as well as Executive Director and Treasurer of the mission.

Unlike most of the outlying mission stations, the parsonage was a huge screened-in residence with electricity and indoor plumbing. Due to the location in a large town with ample shopping and medical facilities, the house was built to be the center for mission conferences, etc. In other words, the 'Mission Hotel'. With five bedrooms and five bathrooms it was constantly full of missionaries in town for shopping or medical care. Over the years more than twenty babies were born in the assorted bedrooms with doctors or midwives in attendance. Then there were also numerous travelers passing through such as the wealthy Americans, contributors to the mission cause, who wanted to see how their money was being spent. In addition to these various interested journalists, teachers on vacation and other exotic types dropped by for a few days.

After the start of World War II, the house became a safe haven for missionaries and diplomats escaping the Japanese occupation of Burma and Thailand. With the construction of American and British airbases in the outskirts of town, the mission house also served as a touch of home for the soldiers with an open house two evenings a week.

Throughout all of this mother was the perfect hostess. With the help of loyal servants she managed to coordinate an efficient and smoothly run operation. Most evenings there were additional guests at our dinner table: new faces with interesting stories to tell.

For us children growing up in the family, it was a fascinating life. Instead of being stuck in some backwoods outpost with few chances to meet other people, we had the opportunity to meet a diverse and interesting variety of individuals. The result was that we learned to take this onslaught of visitors without undue stress. On a few occasions when the house was already filled to the rafters with guests, mother would ask me if I would share my room with some single woman visitor. I can remember a few times of coming home after an evening out at the movies and discovering some strange woman asleep in my full-sized bed. I just crawled in beside her to spend the night with introductions made when we woke in the morning!

As I look back in memory to those childhood days I marvel at the experiences I had. How lucky I was to grow up in the "Mission Hotel" with an endless parade of visitors from every quarter of the earth. What a unique experience.

A STORY NEVER TOLD

It was during those chaotic days of World War ll. For so many people the war caused a traumatic upheaval of the everyday routine of their lives. This was certainly true for the Baptist missionaries who were living and working in Burma. During the years of 1940 and '41 the Japanese had been successful, almost without any resistance, in their goal of dominating and controlling the countries of Southeast Asia and the islands of the Pacific. The organization of the American Baptist mission had a major network of missionaries in Burma, with the central offices in the city of Rangoon.

As the Japanese armies swept through the Indonesian Peninsula and Thailand anyone who could leave Burma did so in a mad scramble to escape before the imminent invasion. Most of the missionaries left in good time but the chief financial officer of the mission, Rev. Kaiser, remained in Rangoon to secure and dispose of the mission's assets. By the time he was ready to leave the invading army was closing in. The airlines as well as shipping had closed down. No motor roads were open to next door India, as the jungles were too dense and the mountains too high for the development of roads. It was essential that he get out of the country as he had converted as much as possible of the mission's assets into cash, which amounted to many hundreds of thousands of dollars. The only way to get to India was to trek out with the help of local tribesmen. He was able to hire a group of back-woodsmen as guides. He stored the cash in a money belt he wore under his clothing night and day. Of course if the men had known he carried all that money they would have murdered him in an instant.

The trek through the jungles and over the mountain passes took three weeks. On one occasion, as they were fording a mountain stream, he was swept downstream. The men had to rescue him, pulling him from the water. His clothes were soaking wet and clinging to his body. He was sure they would discover his money belt and kill him on the spot. However his secret was not discovered and he managed to complete the arduous trek to safety. He arrived at our house to join his wife and son, who had been able to leave Burma by ship at an earlier time. He was greatly relieved, after his harrowing ordeal, to hand the money over into the safe keeping of the mission treasury.

As a footnote to this story, when the war was over and Burma once again was opened to the Baptist missionaries, my dad was asked to go to Rangoon to reestablish the mission complex. He and mother spent their last seven years as missionaries there in Rangoon. The Japanese had used the mission buildings as their headquarters so they were in fairly good condition. However, all the business files and documents had been thrown down a dry well. Fortunately, much was still retrievable which helped with the job of reorganization. This is just one of so many stories about wartime and the havoc it brings to people's lives.

TAKING A FOOLISH CHANCE

In college I majored in Home Economics. My goal was to become a teacher. I attended a state teacher's college in Pennsylvania with an excellent program designed to cover all aspects of the subject. Part of the curriculum was a requirement to spend a semester in a "home management" house situated close to the campus. Six girls at a time lived in the house with a female teacher who was there to supervise and train us in all aspects of managing a home.

In addition to taking our regular classes, we were required to rotate through the jobs necessary to running a household. For a period of ten days we were each responsible for an assignment, such as meal planner, cook, assistant cook, waitress, house cleaner and even nursemaid to a baby borrowed from an orphanage for the school year. But that's a story to tell at another time. The teacher we had was very strict. Each girl was responsible for her own assignment and could not pitch in to help another. We were graded on the quality of our work. When it was my turn to be the cook I was practically a novice. Other than the lab classes in cooking and a few times helping my mother make desserts, I knew nothing about food preparation. A couple of near disasters were the result of my ignorance. The first was in trying to fry calves liver. With not the faintest idea of how long to cook it, the result was inedible. At the first cut bloody juice ran out of the mostly raw liver. Of course that did not go over very well with the teacher. I felt I needed to redeem myself. The next night I was to make a lasagna casserole. All went pretty well. It was to bake for a while in the oven to melt the cheese and set up the noodles combination. Just before time to serve my masterpiece, I reached into the oven to pull out the large casserole; it slid from my grasp and fell to the floor shattering the glass dish into small pieces!

Now what was I to do? No time to start again. However all was not lost, the casserole remained mostly intact. I lifted it carefully up from the floor and laid it on the counter, picking any glass pieces I could see, or feel, from the food. Hoping I had found all the glass pieces I called the other girls aside to warn them to watch for glass in the dish. But of course I couldn't tell the teacher what had happened. As we all sat around the table eating, two or three of us did crunch down on bits of glass. We all watched the teacher with bated breath, hoping for the best. Apparently, she did not encounter any glass in her food. And, in fact, complemented me on the good lasagna. I did manage to get through that assignment without any more mishaps and even successfully passed the course. But as I look back to that incident, I am amazed at how dumb I was. Just imagine what could have happened if someone had swallowed a shard of glass. I must have had an angel watching over my shoulder.

WINTER MAGIC

Having grown up in the tropics I had very little experience with snow. When I came back to America to attend college in Pennsylvania the winters of snow and ice were a new adventure for me. I learned, the hard way, to be extra cautious when walking on an icy sidewalk. I discovered the joy of sledding, and even tried to master ice skating. It was great fun to include the delights and challenges of winter storms in my experiences.

But there is one memory that stands out above most others. It is interesting how a brief experience can make such a vivid and lasting memory. This one has a way of coming back to me whenever I see newly fallen snow. It was during my junior year of college. One evening, as my dormitory roommate and I were studying, I got a phone call from the boy I had been dating. He said he had noticed that there was a fresh snowfall on the ground and thought it would be fun to take a walk in the snow. I agreed, so we met for a late evening walk, bundled in mittens, caps and warm clothing. It was as if we had stepped into another world. Every shrub, tree branch and all else was covered by a piled high blanket of soft, fluffy white snow. The yellow street lights created a golden glow on the whole landscape there was no one else about; we had it all to ourselves, no cars on the street. We could see the glow from windows where other folks were snuggled in for the night. As we walked along the street we made only our tracks in the snow on the sidewalks. There were no sounds. The world was hushed and still. Even our boots made no sound in the soft light snow. We walked along arm in arm without the need to talk. It seems we had found a place of magic. We brought up the idea of making a snowman, but decided it would not fit well into the mood of the night.

Soft flakes of snow drifted down on our shoulders, faces and eyelashes, but it was not cold. We walked for about an hour and saw no another person or vehicle. It was as if we had that glorious world just there for us to share. We stopped by a little cafe for a hot mug of chocolate before parting for the night.

Of course, the next day the magic had gone and the bustle of life resumed. But, somehow, that evening and our walk in the wonderland of snow, has stayed with me throughout all the years—a true moment of magic.

A LABORATORY BABY

For several decades animal lovers and others have been protesting the inhumane and insensitive treatment of animals in laboratories. There are sanctuaries set up for primates to enjoy after being used for tests and experiments. But I have a story to tell about a human baby treated in much the same way. In 1945 I attended a college in Pennsylvania. I was majoring in Home Economics with the intention of becoming a teacher. In addition to the traditional courses relating to foods, nutrition, sewing and science, there was a required course called Home Management. For nine weeks (one half of a semester) six students lived just off campus in a Home Management house with a teacher in residence. The plan was for each student to rotate through a variety of assignments tor a period of ten days each. These were general manager, cook, assistant cook, and grocery shopping, housekeeper and nursery caregiver. For this last duty there was a real, live baby girl provided by a local orphanage for the entire school year of nine months.

During my sophomore year, my turn for residence in the home management house came during the first half of the spring semester. This was in February and March. The baby had been there since September and was eleven months old. We were told there was a strict set of rules to follow. Only the student assigned to the nursery care was allowed to be with the baby; she was responsible for feeding and a daily bath. The baby was brought downstairs for one hour every afternoon to play in the living room, at which time we could all interact with her. Otherwise she stayed in her nursery crib isolated from the rest of us.

In theory, the permanent teacher was supposed to be the surrogate mother, but in this case the teacher was not the motherly type and seldom had anything to do with the lonely and neglected baby. The horror of it all was that the little infant had no one to bond with. From the time of her arrival in September, at the age of three months, she had a steady stream of caretakers for a period of ten days each. I remember hearing her lonely crying for hours. She would stop if she heard footsteps coming up the stairs only to start crying again as no one came into her room. We students hated the rules and if the teacher was not there we would slip into the nursery to hold and comfort the poor little baby. As a result of this monstrous neglect, little Lisa was generally retarded in her development. She spoke very few words. Her motor skills consisted of crawling and standing, but no capacity for walking. She was obviously depressed with little joy or laughter; her world was almost entirely devoid of novelty and stimulation. I don't remember her ever being taken outdoors. As I look back to that time, I am actually horrified at the treatment of that baby. How could child development experts of the day think such use of a baby was justified? The importance of a child's first year when bonding, communication, establishing self worth, being loved and so much more, were totally disregarded! I have no knowledge of how much longer the use of a baby in such a way was continued. At least today we are all aware of the importance of love and bonding as an essential in early child development. In fact, it is hard to believe s such neglect could have taken place by so-called experts such a short time ago.

Through the years I have often wondered how little Lisa turned out. For her, and many other infants, subjected to such a horrific first year, it was an unforgivable beginning. I do hope she was able to overcome the abuse and find love and joy in her life.

DONALD—THE DUCK

We were living with my aunt and grandmother and I was ten years old. It was Easter time and my parents had a wonderful surprise for me. They brought home a cut little duckling for me as a pet. Of course I had to name him Donald after the cartoon character. He was adorable with his tiny webbed feet and little bill; he was a tiny ball of yellow fluff.

He had the run of the house. It was not long before he discovered that grandma kept the lettuce and other greens on the bottom shelf of the refrigerator. Whenever he would see grandma going to open the fridge door he would be right there to hop onto the shelf to get a little quick snack!

For his daily bath we would put a few inches of water into the bathtub. Donald had a wonderful time swimming around and ducking under the water to get completely wet. My aunt Jean was so delighted with his antics that when any company came to visit she would take him out of his sleeping cage (day or night), fill a basin with water to show off his bath routine.

He had imprinted on me. He would follow me everywhere in the yard; he even would follow me down the sidewalk, waddling along behind, even when we went downtown.

But Donald did not stay small for long. Within a few months he began to lose his baby down, replaced with white feathers. His chirps turned into loud quacks. Worst of all, he began to leave his poop everywhere. We built him a large fenced in pen in the backyard. He was now a full-grown white duck who did a lot of loud quacking. The neighbors began to complain about the noise and pooping.

We figured out a solution. There was a nice duck pond on the outskirts of town. One afternoon we took our pet, Donald, over to that pond to join the other ducks there. For several months after his release we came by for a visit. We would call his name and he would waddle over to say hello and get some pets.

Many years later when I had young children of my own I wanted them to have that same experience. We bought two little ducklings, one for each of my two boys. It was great fun to watch them go through all the same antics. I did make one compromise to their living situation. We very soon made a nice penned in enclosure for them with their own little pond. I was quite impressed with the tolerant attitude my aunt and grandmother had shown for my own little ducking in the matter of pooping all over the house.

When those two ducklings grew up and began to poop everywhere we also had a plan. We lived in San Diego, the home of a world famous zoo. We had noticed they had a pond of exotic ducks from around the world. One late evening we took our two ordinary duck pets and threw them over the high fence near the entrance to the zoo. On later visits to the zoo we looked for out duck friends, we had no luck. Perhaps the zoo keepers didn't want to take on the care of ordinary ducks—I really can't blame them.

THE BRITISH RAJ

Let me say, before I begin this story, that what I relate here are just the memories of a teenager living in India during the last days of British rule! I am not an historian. I am sure that what I remember is just a very small part of the total story of what took place during the years of British occupation.

It all started more than 200 years ago; England had impressive dominance of the oceans of the world. Much of their wealth was due to their dependency on world trade. The East India Company was formed to facilitate an efficient means to develop trade in regions of the Far East. India had a vast supply of desirable goods for trade, such as textiles, spices, exotic woods and jewels, to mention just a few. It was of benefit to both sides to open up channels of trade.

At that time most of India was divided into small principalities ruled by a royal family. The ruler was called a Rajah; his wife called a Ranee. Hence the term "British Raj" refers to the British Rule of India. These rulers, for the most part, had accumulated great wealth by the labor of their subjects. It was fairly easy for the East India Company to persuade these rulers to join into trade agreements, which benefited both sides. For the most part, all this was done without conflict. It was only after the British government took over with the establishment of garrisons of soldiers to protect British interests, that the

Indians woke up to the fact that they had become a colony under British rule.

The stories written by Kipling, and others, tell of some of the Indian efforts to revolt and drive the British out of India. One such revolt includes the story of "The Black Hole of Calcutta", a famous event in History. The way the story goes a rebel force was able to capture some 300 British soldiers. They were forced to spend overnight locked up in a 20 foot by 30 foot room. The only ventilation was a small skylight. There was no room to sit down; the men were packed together in a standing position. When morning came, almost two-thirds of the soldiers had died during the night from the intense heat and lack of air. I visited this room when I was child; it is now a memorial to the horrific episode.

In return, there are incidents where the British also were involved in genocide of whole villages of people as a way to quell uprisings. This all took place long before my parents came to India as missionaries. The revolts had subsided and things were relatively peaceful.

One interesting aspect during the period of British rule in India, which lasted some 200 years, is the story of the Northwest frontier. This was the part of India now the western regions of Pakistan. This whole region was, and still is to this day, occupied and controlled by fierce, extremely hostile, tribes competing for wealth and power. This is the same area along the Afghanistan-Pakistani border where the Taliban leaders are successful in holding off the armies of Pakistan and the United States. This region has never been conquered by any foreign power.

When the British ruled India they never had control of that mountainous, remote area. The Khyber Pass, the only road from Afghanistan into the whole Indian sub-continent, runs right through the center of the region. It is the same pass through which Alexander the Great and many other conquering armies of the past, and migrations of people who came to India from the West.

During the time of the British a deal was made with these tribes. Each tribe, living in fortified walled villages, was given an annual bribe of several hundred rupees to allow safe passage on the Khyber Pass Road. The story goes that any traveler is only protected on the road. Travelers had to camp and stay right on the road itself. If one strayed, even a foot or two, off the road they would be fair game for sharp shooters from the surrounding hills.

Even to this day the Pakistani government has limited control over the region of the Khyber Pass. On my visit back to Pakistan in 1992 we hired a bus to take us on the Khyber Pass Road to go as far as the border of Afghanistan. A Pakistani soldier accompanied us carrying a high-powered rifle. We were told not to get out of the bus while traveling the Road, as we might be the targets for a sharpshooter hiding in the surrounding hills. We passed by villages still protected by high walls. Women were working in the wheat fields near the villages. We saw the remains of a British fort and a memorial plaque dedicated to the British officers killed in the conflict with the tribesmen of the region. We could only take pictures from the windows of the bus. After about a 2 to 3 hour drive we arrived at the border of Afghanistan, there we were able to get off the bus. At that time Russians were still trying to take over Afghanistan. We saw evidence of mortar fire where the Russians had battled with the Afghan military only three days before we got there. We all did have the feeling that the war was just a little too close for comfort!

It seems the welfare of the people of India was promoted by the British, but only to the extent of improving and facilitating trade. They established a fine railroad system, but did nothing to improve the roads or motorized vehicles. They promoted the education of the children of the wealthy, even sending them to England for college degrees, in order to develop a stable structure of lower level government officials, but did little in the way of educating the rest of the population. In my period in India, the literacy rate was under 10%.

The establishment of a strong army was top priority. All the officers were British, but the recruitment of native troops, with good reliable pensions, was well organized. Any healthy young man could have an army career with the prospect of a comfortable retirement. The policy for helping out in matters of education, medical care and religious conversion were left to missionaries. The British encouraged mission workers from England and America. Missionaries were present throughout the Indian subcontinent; each denomination was given a territory to establish schools, medical clinics and churches, thus developing a system to improve the lives of the people without involvement of the British government. These missions came into existence as far back as the early 1800s.

There was another consequence of the British presence in India. The British army officers and government officials were given assignments to be in India for five to ten year duties with furloughs home to England on a regular schedule. Many of those men opted to leave their wives and families back in England where life was much more civilized. As a result, as men will be men, it was not uncommon for these men to take on any Indian "wife". As a result, a large population of "Anglo-Indian" children came into existence. After several generations there were many Anglo-Indian communities throughout India. There were proud of their British blood and lived and dressed as Englishmen. My father was a minister to an Anglo-Indian congregation.

In 1947, when India finally got their independence from British rule, the nation wanted to get rid of anything British. The Anglo-Indian population no longer felt welcome with their British blood; large groups have emigrated to counties all over the world. I have a dear Anglo-Indian childhood friend from India who moved to the United States. She speaks of the tragedy of a scattered ethnic group who no longer has an identity or connection.

In the 1940s as World War II was in full swing, the Japanese had taken over most of the Pacific and conquered Burma—the next door neighbor to India. There was a real possibility that they would plan an invasion of India. As a safeguard, British and American troops flooded into East India to prevent this from happening. The Americans set up three airfields to send bombers to Burma and even as far as China. There were some 50 thousand American troops and another 75 thousand British and Australian troops in the area. (The dreaded invasion never came; perhaps the Japanese had their hands full fighting the Americans in the Islands of the Pacific!) A large percentage of the British troops were made up of the native population with British officers in the higher ranks.

I remember one incident that took place during this time. A couple of high ranking British officers got drunk one weekend and went looking for women to rape in a small Indian village on the outskirts of the town I lived in. When the officers turned up missing, there was a search made in the village. Their decapitated heads were found in the village well. In total disregard for what the British officers had done the village was given 12 hours to evacuate and then the village was burned to the ground. This was the only time I saw the injustice of the British power.

This is the time when Gandhi was trying to gain independence for India. With his methods of passive resistance and hunger strikes, the British, fearing an uprising of the population, promised that after the war was over they would grant independence. Gandhi never saw that day. He was assassinated by a disgruntled Hindu man who felt Gandhi was a pawn of the British rulers. The tragedy of the story is what took place during the negotiations. Jinnha was the leader of the Muslim delegation. He was fearful that Muslims, a minority of the population, would not have a strong vote in the establishment of a democratic government. He insisted that all the provinces, with a majority of Muslims break away to form a separate country named Pakistan. These provinces were mostly in the Northwest part of India. They were the result of the time when India was ruled by Muslim conquerors. However, there was one province away in the central far eastern part of India. This was the province of Bangladesh with a Muslim majority. In the middle 1940s, as plans for the establishment of two countries was being worked out, total chaos broke out. Hindus, Muslims and Christians who had been living in harmony, without any major problems, suddenly felt the need to move and establish a new home in the country of their own religion. This meant the upheaval of thousands of families. Old hatreds and fears broke out and the killing began. We heard stories of families traveling by train: as the train passed through Muslim held territory, the Muslims would come aboard and kill all the Hindus on the train. The same thing took place as the train passed through Hindu territory. The only ones spared were the Christians who were considered neutral. The province of Bengal was close to even between Hindus and Muslims. The major city of Calcutta was the same way. One terrible day the opposing forces met on a bridge in the center of the city, hundreds of people were slaughtered and their bodies thrown off the bridge into the river below. The river ran red with blood! Independence finally came in 1947 with the establishment of two countries, India and Pakistan. But even today, some 70 years later, the distrust and fear permeates both countries. India has had much success in developing an educated society with a strong middle class. However, Pakistan has not been so fortunate. They have had numerous takeovers by military leadership. They also have the problem of thousands of refugees from Afghanistan and the disgruntled Taliban occupies their northeast borders. Poor little Bangladesh, being so isolated from the rest of Pakistan, was unable to maintain ties to Pakistan and in a few years became a separate nation. It is desperately poor and having great difficulty surviving. Also there is one other province of Kashmir that is still a part of India, even though it had a majority of Muslims. Nehru, the first prime minister of India, came from Kashmir. He insisted that it remain a part of India. Even up to the present time, the two countries are fighting over the territory.

Most historians agree that the breakup of India into two separate countries was a tragic mistake. The Muslims who remained in India, and the Hindus who remained in Pakistan, have found a way to get along with their neighbors, even though they are a small minority. The over 200 years of British rule in India did much to bring that nation into the modern world. From a nation divided up into small principalities into a well functioning democratic nation. There is one interesting sideline to the story of India gaining their independence. The Indians were eager to rid themselves of everything British. However, when trying to set up a generalized government, they ran into a language problem. There are some 40 different languages spoken throughout India, from the time of the principalities that existed before the British came. Many of the local government officials already spoke English. The only logical solution was to make English the universal language of India. It was a bitter pill to swallow!

When I was a child growing up in India, one couldn't get along without some knowledge of the local language. All the shopkeepers, waiters and general population spoke no English. When I returned on a visit to India in the 1980s, I was amazed at the use of English everywhere we went. It is now taught in every school as a second language.

The period between the fifteenth century and the twentieth century was a time of exploration. The countries of Europe didn't even know the American continent existed. The ships were capable of traveling the oceans of the world. Routes were established to bring the exotic goods from anywhere on earth. Less advanced societies were looked down on as being inferior. Slavery was prevalent throughout the world. Just consider how we treated the Native Americans when we were taking over lands they had occupied for thousands of years. The British were not alone in their desire to accumulate wealth. It was simply the attitude of nations at that time in history.

In 1947 when India gained her independence I was in college in Pennsylvania. After graduating from high school in 1944, I left India in 1945 to return to America and the protective arms of my grandmother. My parents left India in 1947 during the joyous celebration of independence. They served one last seven-year term in the mission field, but they did not return to India. The mission board felt they would be of more use in Burma to reestablish the mission work there. The mission headquarters was in Rangoon. The Japanese had established their army command on the grounds of the mission. As my dad found out, they had not destroyed all of the mission records, they were found discarded in a dry well. After serving their last term in Rangoon they retired after 25 years in the mission field in India and Burma.

— Years 20 to 40 —

ALL FOR A
GOOD NIGHT'S SLEEP

We have all had times when our sleep has been disturbed by some sort of loud noise. I can recall a Couple of instances when this occurred many years ago when I was married to my first husband, Pete. We were newlyweds and I was not accustomed to sharing my bed. One night I had a vivid dream in which I was being chased through the forest by a ferocious bear. I spotted a large log and managed to wedge myself up against the log and pull fallen leaves and debris over me. The bear started to sniff around close by and was on the verge of discovering my hiding place.

Just at that perilous moment, Pete sat up in bed to see the time on the clock by the bed. Thinking he was the bear in my dream, I reached out and slammed him with my outstretched arm knocking him back down flat on his pillow. The action woke me as I hit him, but the damage was already done! I'm sure he must have wondered what kind of wild woman he had married. It took lots of apologies to make it right.

A couple of years later we were living in a small cottage at the rear of our landlady's property. I woke one night to find Pete in the process of changing his pajamas. When I asked him why, he said it was because they were wet. That really peaked my curiosity, as I couldn't imagine such a thing. He then told me what had happened. He had awakened to the yowling of a tomcat sitting on a fence right outside our kitchen window. Pete slipped into the kitchen and quietly filled a large pot with cold water. Thinking the window glass was open, he threw the whole pan full of water out the window, hoping to have it land on the cat. However, much to his shock and surprise, the window was not open and the water all came back on him, drenching him completely. We both had a good laugh, while the old tomcat kept on yowling outside the window.

Years later we had bought a home in the suburbs of San Diego. There was a large tall elm tree in the back yard. At the front of the house stood a tall pole with a streetlight at the top. A mockingbird took up residence in the elm tree. We enjoyed his loud, melodic songs throughout the day. However, this musical bird did not confine his singing to daylight. Each night he would wake up around 2 AM and see the streetlight shining over the house roof into the top of his tree. Thinking it must be dawn, he would start his noisy singing. It was so loud we would not be able to sleep. Pete tried everything from yelling out the window to throwing anything handy up into the tree with no success. One night, to my amusement, he even tried wrapping his arms around the trunk of the large elm tree in an attempt to shake the massive tree.

Finally, after nights of frustration, one day Pete had had enough. He got out his twenty-two rifle and took aim at the mockingbird perched at the top of the light pole. He came close, but missed hitting the bird. But it did solve the problem. Our musical tormentor must have decided he had worn out his welcome and moved his roost off to another neighborhood, leaving us to nights of peaceful sleep.

LOVE CONQUERS ALL

When that basic urge of nature to procreate calls, it seems both man and beast cannot resist. Herein are two stories when, despite the efforts of their owners, doggy love found a way!

The first story is about our neighbor who lived directly beyond our back yard. A five-foot solid wood fence separated our yards. She had two beautiful thoroughbred female miniature white poodles which were her pride and joy. She had spent a great deal of money to purchase these gorgeous little dogs and hoped to profit by selling their pedigreed puppies.

In the neighborhood we also had a free roving dog named "Taco". He was the result of some very unfortunate breeding. He was a combination of Dachshund in his long fat body and stubby short legs, but his head was that of a German Sheppard, too large for that squat body. Probably one of the ugliest dogs l have ever seen. It happened that both lovely poodle females came into heat at the same time. This was too much for Taco to resist! I observed, with some wicked delight, (as my neighbor was a bit of a snob) as Taco diligently spent more than an hour digging a hole under the fence to join the two eager little ladies. It wasn't until the deed had been accomplished that my neighbor discovered the unwanted visitor and threw him out of her yard. After the appropriate time had elapsed the result of this illicit encounter produced the weirdest little puppies imaginable; short squat bodies, oversized heads and tan curly fur. They were even worse looking than Taco.

The other story is about a lovely little Beagle who was the pet of Phil, the principle at the school where l was a teacher. One day he posted a notice in the teacher's lounge stating that he had four Beagle puppies to give away. He then told us how it was that his beloved little pet Beagle had gotten pregnant. When she came into heat he did not want her to mate. The family was all being extra careful to not let that happen. One night, just as they were sitting down for dinner, they heard a scratching at the front door. When Phil went to investigate he was upset to find their dog standing there waiting to enter. After letting her in she headed right for the back rooms of the house. Phil bawled out his kids for being so careless as to let the dog outside alone.

As they were finishing dinner, out of the bedrooms trotted two very happy dogs. They were almost identical in appearance, as most beagles are. So that is why Phil had some cute little puppies available. He did enjoy telling how it all came about. He had actually invited the smart little male into the rendezvous of love.

A DIFFERENT POINT OF VIEW

Having grown up in India with a multi-racial and cultural society, I can honestly say that I have no racial prejudice. My parents taught us that all people on earth are the same under the color of their skin.

The nursemaid who cared for me as a small child was a sweet and loving Indian woman. She spoke no English, but wrapped me in her love and care. In my memory, I can still smell her aroma of coconut and sandalwood.

Years later as a prospective teacher in San Diego, my first assignment as a student teacher was in a mostly African-American junior high school. I was home economics major and this was a sewing and foods class. At first the all girl class of students was reserved and cautious. But as time passed and they felt my warmth and acceptance, they became open and friendly. In fact, at Christmas time that class gave me more gifts and cards than any other class in my twenty four years of teaching.

One day, as the whole class was crowded around my desk, I was showing them how to make fabric covered cording. One of the girls passed wind with a loud prolonged whine. In my past experience, when such a thing happened among white girls there would be no reaction, especially in the presence of a teacher. Only embarrassment and a few muffled giggles. But this was not the case here.

One of the other students demanded in a loud voice, "who just farted?" This broke the tension and the girls all laughed, including me.

Later on in the school year I was in the foods curriculum. I was giving a demonstration on how one should set a table. I was explaining the correct position for knives, forks and spoons at each place setting. I began to sense some tension in the class. Finally, one girl raised her hand to speak. She said she was confused, because in their home all the utensils were put in a large jar in the center of the table. If someone wanted a fork, they just took it out of the jar, Etc. No fuss or bother with table setting!

My reaction was in agreement; I said I thought that was an excellent way to set the table. But I suggested that later on when they were married, and wanted to have their husband's boss and wife over for dinner, they might want to show that they knew how to set a proper table. This seemed to make sense to them, so they all became interested in the project.

We do have so much to learn from others. Just because that's the way we learned to do something, it doesn't mean that it is the only way, or even the best way. Our openness to new ideas can be a way to gain knowledge and perspective in the way we live together, with tolerance and understanding for others and their way of life.

THE TROPHY

It seems to be something that runs in the blood, this passion for fishing. I suspect it develops early in life. My first husband, Pete, had this passion. For a period of ten years he was a commercial tuna fisherman out of San Diego. But, even that time of constant fishing did not decrease his love of the pastime. Then from the time our two sons could hold a fishing pole they were instructed on the techniques required to be successful in the art of fishing. I can't recall a time when fishing was not a part of our camping trips. On the other hand, I never caught the fishing bug. I enjoying catching fish but not the hours spent waiting for a fish to take the bait.

When Gary, our oldest son, was sixteen and Dave twelve, their dad died after a long illness. I wanted to continue in the family camping traditions so two years later we planned a fishing trip during summer vacation. Gary had a job and decided he would need to stay home. To make the trip more fun for Dave he invited a friend of his, Donny, to come along. Thinking that I would probably need a little break from the company of two fourteen-year olds, I invited my mother, aged seventy-five, to join us. She was not much of a camper, but a good sport and willing to give it a try.

I rented a truck with a slide-on camper. It was a pretty cozy arrangement; mother and l would sleep in the cab-over bed, while Dave and his buddy would sleep in the bed converted from the dining nook. We said our farewells to Gary and headed on up to the Yuba River in northern California. We got as far as San Francisco where we stopped for a short visit with my brother, Stan, and his family. While there we got a call from Gary. The thought of missing out on our adventure was more that he could bear; he quit his job and joined us. His excuse was that he felt I should have some help with the driving! So now our little camper was even cozier. The only place left for Gary to sleep was the small space on the door. It made a challenging obstacle course for anyone needing to visit the bathroom during the night. We had timed our visit to coincide with the Yuba river steelhead run. For those readers unfamiliar with steelhead, they are a species of freshwater salmon that migrate upstream to spawn. Upon our arrival we found the campground rather crowded with lots of avid fishermen already lined up along the riverbank to try their luck. Gary, Dave and Donny soon had their lines in the water with all the rest.

The day did not go well, a few steelhead could be seen working their way up through the riffles and rapids, but few were being caught. However, this did not deter the eager fishermen who patiently waited for their moment of success. The day went by. None of the boys had any luck. The sun began to slip below the treetops; it was about time to leave the river and head back to camp.

It was then that it happened. Dave hooked onto a big one! As it fought, and leaped out of the water, it was plain to see it was, indeed, a monster! The great fish was eager to break free and charged up and down the river, making Dave follow, scrambling over rocks and bushes. That was when a remarkable thing happened. All the other fishermen, seeing the size of the fish, reeled in their lines to give Dave a clear place to pull in his grand trophy. The battle between the boy and fish continued for about thirty minutes. When, at last Dave pulled the exhausted fish up on the riverbank all the other fishermen came over to admire the fish and congratulate Dave. It was, by far, the biggest steelhead caught that day. Back at camp we enjoyed the fish fry and had plenty left to share with other campers.

Dave, even to this day, at the age of sixty, likes nothing better than spending the day fishing. Of course!

THE ELUSIVE GRUNION

Living in San Diego had some wonderful advantages. It is true that other places in the country have the refreshing change of seasons which are missing in southern California. To watch the fresh green of spring and the glorious colors of fall are a real joy. But Southern California makes up for it with almost continuously sunny, balmy weather throughout most of the year. For anyone who loves outdoor activities, an ideal place to live.

One of the time honored activities for those who love the ocean beaches is grunion hunting. Now for those poor deprived folks who are unlucky enough to live in states to the east, the common belief is that grunion hunting and snipe hunting are in the same category of myth. It is true that sometimes those little grunions never do show up when expected and the whole excursion degenerates into just a good old beach party of hot dogs and beer.

But now it is time to explain a bit about grunion. They are a little herring type fish six to ten inches long. During the summer nights, at full moon, the high tides are the signal for them to propagate. If all is right, they wash in on the tidal waves by the hundreds onto the flat beaches. In the brief time between waves, the female stands up on her tail to brush a hollow in the sand, then lays her eggs. The male grunion, which has been close by, fertilizes the eggs. All this happens before the next wave washes sand over the eggs and carries the fish back out to sea. Quite an amazing accomplishment. If all went well, the eggs would hatch into fish to be carried out with the next month's high tides. For the grunion hunter it is just a matter of running up the beach to catch the wiggling fish by hand before they swim out with the next wave. On several occasions I have seen hundreds of fish on each high tidal wave. One could collect a bucketful in half an hour.

However, as grunion hunting became more popular the fish started to wise up. According to the naturalists, the fish are starting to avoid coming up on the beaches where there are lights from cars and campfires. They are finding more secluded areas. By the period of the 1980's it was only rarely we were able to find grunion. So what did we do with the grunion we caught? The tried and true procedure was as follows: First, rinse them well in clean ocean water. Pat them dry, then dip the whole fish; head, tail and all, into batter and crumbs. You need to have a good fire going and a heavy cast-iron skillet to fry them in. To eat them you hold the fish by the head and tail and nibble off the meat from the backbone, leaving the guts, head and tail. They were pretty good: it was mostly the flavor of the breading that you tasted. I think the real fun of it all was the main attraction. It made us all feel like little kids again, chasing down those little silver fishes!

COUSIN FRANK

Frank, and his older brother Jack, were the children of my mother's youngest sister, Hester. She was married to a college professor but died of a strep throat infection when Frank was only two years old. His father remarried, and the boys were raised in a loving, stable home in the college town of Franklin, Indiana. Having spent my childhood in India, I only saw Jack and Frank two or three times as children. As time went by I married and moved to San Diego and had two children, Gary and David. My father died and my mother and her one remaining sister Jean, moved from Pennsylvania to San Diego to be close to me and our little family. They bought a small modest house close by. Frank, in the meantime, graduated from college. The Korean War was in progress and so he decided to join the marines and was sent to Korea. After the conflict ended and he was discharged, he was unsure of where he wanted to go or what he wanted to do. He dropped by San Diego to visit his two elderly aunts. On finding such a cozy little nest he asked if he could live with them for a while until he could determine what he wanted to do. They were delighted and flattered to think he would ask to stay with them. This unusual arrangement seemed to work out remarkably well. Frank was in his late twenties, full of energy and testosterone.

Our family was delighted to have him close by. Gary and Dave were in their preteens and loved to have a big macho fun loving cousin to share in their activities. We also enjoyed his telling us stories in his slow midwestern drawl. He became a welcome addition to our campouts and adventures. It is hard to imagine how he fit in with his two elderly aunts nightly games of scrabble and far from exciting lifestyle. But it seems they all got along quite well. However, on occasion, Frank did have the urge to kick up his heels, and the Mexican border town of Tijuana was not far away. There he could spend a little time doing what young men like to do. On one such excursion on a Saturday night, he met a quite lovely and friendly Mexican senorita in a bar. Things were progressing nicely, with suggestive advances going both ways, when suddenly a furious, knife wielding boyfriend rushed into the bar and headed straight towards them.

Frank decided the quickest avenue of escape was out the back door. He spotted a ladder leading up to a flat roof of a nearby house. He spent the rest of the night flattened on the rooftop while the angry man and his friends searched the streets for the "gringo". As daylight dawned at last, it seemed safe to go back to his car. He arrived home just as his not too happy aunts were leaving for church. That did manage to put a little frost between them for a few days. I remember two incidents when Frank was with our family. One was on a campout in the desert. We had started a campfire to help with the morning's chill. As we were standing around the fire Pete (my husband) saw an ember pop out of the fire and land on Frank's shirt which was hung on a close by chair. He yelled at Frank, "your shirts on fire". In an instant, much to the hilarious laughter of all of us watching, Frank flung himself to the ground and started rolling over and over while his smoldering shirt on the chair was ignored.

Another time we were having a late night barbeque on the beach. During the summer months the balmy weather on the beaches in southern California is irresistible. We had finished our meal and thought it would be nice to have a campfire. However, the wood we had brought didn't seem to catch fire very well. Not to worry, Pete had brought along a glass jar full of gasoline for just that sort of problem. The procedure was to sprinkle some gas on a few sticks of wood and then tuck them into the fire to help ignite the slow burning pile. But before that could take place, Frank the macho marine, grabbed the jar of gasoline and proceeded to pour a stream right onto the bonfire! The result was instantaneous! The fire immediately raced back up the stream of gas to the bottle. Thankfully, Frank reacted at once and flung the bottle away into the sand. The flame quickly burned out with no harm done. However, Frank did have to take a lot of ribbing about his fire building skills.

It took a few months for Frank to figure out what he wanted to do with his future. He was offered a position as the Dean of Students at Syracuse University. He was also looking for a girl with some depth of personality. He not only found his direction for a career, but also met and married the girl of his dreams, Isabel, a girl from Scotland. They have raised four children and are living "happily ever after". But Frank's brief time, when he was a part of our lives, is also a happy memory.

A MATTER OF LIFE AND DEATH

It was the summer of 1950. We were living in San Diego. One of our favorite activities was to spend time at the beach. We discovered the beautiful, un-crowded beaches along the coast of Mexico were within an easy distance of thirty to forty miles, and, well worth the effort. One beautiful sunny weekend we decided to take a two-day trip into Mexico and stay in a motel at Rosarita Beach, a drive of about forty miles. Our son, Gary, was a year old so we didn't opt for camping on the beach. After getting checked into the motel we headed out to find a good beach for surfing on our inner tubes. I think this was before the time when surfboards had become popular. A few miles south of town we found a lovely long beach of white sand and impressive waves tumbling onto the shore. We were delighted to see we were completely alone with the whole beach to ourselves. We set up the playpen for the baby with a big beach umbrella to protect him from too much sun. Then we headed off into the surf with our inner tubes to catch a few waves. My husband, Pete, was wearing a pair of flippers, but I didn't have any and soon discovered the waves were just too strong and powerful for me to get out past the breakers. I told Pete that he should go ahead and that I was going back to shore.

It was about then that I started to get into trouble. I found I was being pulled along by a strong undercurrent parallel to the shore. I was a fairly good swim-mer (I had earned a life saving badge in a college swim program). But I found I was unable to move towards the more shallow water closest to shore. I was in water about twelve feet deep. The waves were crashing down on top of me with such force that each successive wave would slam the inner tube from my grasp and smash me to the ocean floor. Over and over again I would just be able to reach the inner tube only to be knocked loose with the next huge wave.

Pete was completely unaware that I was in serious trouble. By this time I was some distance from him and out of his sight. It was about this time that I had the thought that I really might not make it! I seemed to be completely power-less to escape the monstrous waves. I thought I just couldn't let that happen, for I had so much to live for with my dear little baby who needed his mommy!

Finally, after fighting with all my strength, I was able to get into more shallow water where the waves were not as powerful When I finally managed to crawl up onto the beach, I lay there for several minutes, totally exhausted, but so very grateful to be alive.

It was a lesson on how easy it is to find that death is really not very far away. He can come along almost anytime he chooses. But that day was not his day to win!

YOU'RE FIRED

It wasn't that I had no experience of waiting on tables. During my college years I worked as a waitress in the dining room to offset my room and board, I also waited tables for a couple of summers at a church related retreat facility in Green Lake, Wisconsin. But, as I discovered, that was no training for being a waitress in a real restaurant.

I was a newly wed. We rented a small apartment in San Diego. One of our favorite eating-out spots was the nearby chicken pie restaurant. I was a little bored with nothing to do, so I thought I might like to apply for a waitress job there. When I told the owner about my previous experience he seemed to be a little dubious. He suggested that I start out in the back dining room where things were not so busy. I very soon discovered it was not as easy as it looked. The procedure was that after taking the food order the waitress went into the kitchen to call out the order to the cook. Now this cook was a crabby old man. He had his own lingo for each food order. For instance you didn't just ask for "one chicken pot pie". You had to say, "One chicken under cover". I f you didn't say it exactly like he wanted he would give you a cold stare and ignore your requests. This was true for every single item on the menu. I had to keep a notepad in mu pocket to check on how to give each order.

Besides all that, when things were slow in my section of the restaurant, I was expected to help out in the kitchen washing pots and pans. Not the best way to stay fresh and tidy. I managed somehow, to work through these difficulties. I had been working there for about ten days when the boss presented me with the ultimate test. His wife and three friends sat down in my dining area to be served. All four ordered soup for a starter. In my past experience I could have used a tray but not here. Each bowl of soup came on a saucer. The trick was to stack two bowls in each hand, one on top of another. As I tried to set them down on the table one bowl of hot soup slid off the saucer spilling hot soup all over the boss's wife. With much confusion we all managed to clean up the mess. As I finished my work for the day, and went to the boss for my paycheck, I anticipated the worst. Before he could say, "you're fired!" I thought I would beat him to it with the announcement that I would quit. I never did try to be a waitress again. But I do have a great admiration for the job they do! As I found out, it is not all that easy after all!

WITNESS TO A MIRACLE

It was while pulling weeds in our back yard that I came across a chrysalis (the cocoon of a butterfly) attached to a tall weed. Not having any idea of what kind of butterfly would emerge, I thought it would be interesting to find out. I gently cut the weed off at ground level and propped it up in a tall glass in our kitchen Window. I checked it often for any signs of movement. Several days passed. Then finally one morning, I observed some activity. As I watched, the cocoon began to jerk around. Soon I saw a split developing down the entire length. What backed out of the opening didn't look anything like a butterfly. It resembled a wet, lumpy worm with long spindly legs and antenna. I was holding the weed in my hand to get a closer look. The little insect started to make its way down the stem and right onto my hand on unsure, wobbly legs. It proceeded to walk up my arm trying to find a high point for eventual flight. I transferred it onto my other hand which I held up high. I could see its wings crumpled up against its body. Gradually the wings began to unfurl, with each flap they became more infused with the body fluids. What had once been wet, crumpled appendages, turned into glorious wings of brilliant orange and black? It was a Monarch with a wingspan of four to five inches, one of the most beautiful of butterflies.

It took about fifteen minutes for the wings to fully develop, and then as if it had always known how to fly, it fluttered off across the room. It was strange to have this beautiful little creature indoors. It soon found the nearest window to escape to the sunny world outdoors. I put out my finger and it obligingly climbed on my hand. I went outside to let my new little friend fly away to join the others of its kind.

The Monarch butterfly is in decline. Apparently the only plant the caterpillar will eat is milkweed, so with the expansion of agriculture the milkweed is less abundant. This is the same butterfly, which spends the winter months in Central Mexico. They gather by the billions to cover the forest trees in a solid blanket of orange and black. It's a truly amazing journey for such a fragile creature.

Although I had seen numerous TV programs showing the transformation of a cocoon to a butterfly, it was a remarkable experience to be so closely involved; to be a witness to one of the miracles of nature.

THAT OLD DEMON RUM

As a child growing up, our family was strictly a household of teetotalers. My parents were a part of the prohibition era. My father was a minister and mother, at one time, was president of a local chapter of the WCTU (Women's Christian Temperance Union). My two brothers and I were told of the evils that came from the use of alcohol. It was imperative that one never takes a drink, as that would probably lead to a drunken addiction.

My first transgression occurred when I was a student in college. I was on a dinner date with two other couples. Everyone was ordering a before dinner drink. Not wanting to stand out as a wimp, I ordered a glass of blackberry wine (not very appropriate for a pre-dinner cocktail). As I took my first sip I remember thinking that might mean I would possibly become a hopeless alcoholic. That didn't happen, so through the years I have enjoyed the moderate consumption of beer, wine and the occasional cocktail. My two brothers also "fell off the wagon" of the nondrinker. However, if my mother was present, I would find myself full of uncomfortable guilt. On one occasion my mother,

Fred and I were picking up my brother, Stan, from the airport. It was the dinner hour so we stopped at a restaurant on our way home. The waiter asked if we would like to have a drink before ordering dinner. Stan said that would be fine and ordered a cocktail. Fred also selected a cocktail and I, feeling quite guilty, ordered a glass of red wine. This was a shocking event for mother. She, of course, declined with an air of strong disapproval. Whereupon Stan, in his most congenial voice announced "but mother, it is so civilized".

I, on the other hand, felt so uncomfortable drinking in front of mother, that I spilled some of the red wine on my white dress. Mother's terse comment was, "See what happens when you are drunk?" But I did discover another side to my mother's attitude about alcohol. We were invited to a baby shower for a dear friend of mine. As refreshments were being served, mother was quite pleased with the taste of the punch. She asked for a couple of refills. One of my friends, knowing mother's history, whispered to me that the punch contained a good proportion of rum. When I gave mother that information, she didn't even blink an eye. She replied, with no sign of distress, that because she hadn't known she was drinking alcohol, it was perfectly all right. However, she did decline another glass of the stuff.

Of course that all happened many years ago. I do appreciate that for some people, alcohol can be a serious problem. But for me, I do admit a glass of wine does smooth out the day. Perhaps a feeling of being just a little naughty adds a bit to the pleasure!

THE MERMAID SHOW

According to several magazines San Diego has one of the Best climates to be found anywhere on earth. Even though it is situated in the far south, the proximity to the ocean tempers the climate year round. Even on the hottest days of summer cool ocean breezes moderate the temperature. I was fortunate to have lived almost fifty years of my adult life in that area. One of our favorite pastimes was going to the Beaches. There are numerous choices, from gentle bayside spots (ideal for small children) to long stretches of sandy shores with rolling breakers perfect for body surfing and surfboarding. One place we loved to go was the beach at La Jolla Cove.

La Jolla is a beautiful small town just north of San Diego. It is popular with the rich and famous. The downtown streets are lined with high priced boutiques and fancy restaurants. The coastline is made up of rocky coves and sea caves. The city park overlooks a breakwater composed of rugged natural rock that curves around to form a quiet bay with a crescent of sandy beach. It is a perfect place to swim and relax on the white sand. We discovered the rocky breakwater was a wonderful place to snorkel as it is full of exotic colorful sea life and hidden underwater caves to explore. With calm, clear water an ideal place to spend an afternoon.

One sunny summer day my husband and I, with another couple who also enjoyed snorkeling, made plans to spend the day at La Jolla cove. The beach was crowded with sunbathers enjoying the perfect setting. There were also several people snorkeling on the breakwater rocks across from the beach crowd, some two hundred feet across the small bay. It didn't take us long to set up our blankets on the beach and get our facemasks on to begin snorkeling. We were having a wonderful time diving down to find many starfish, small octopus, and bright orange garibaldi fish looking like oversized goldfish. The ledge of rocks above the water was a place to rest and catch your breath. After one of my dives I was having some difficulty climbing out of the water onto the ledge. My husband and another man were resting on the ledge when they saw my predicament and reached down to help. They each grabbed one arm and lifted me up out of the water. My swimsuit had a single strap that went around my neck. As they pulled me up the strap broke and my swimsuit slipped down to my waist exposing my top half for all the world to see. I hung there, it seemed to me, for several minutes of total embarrassment before my "helpers" saw what had happened and let go of my hands. I dropped back into the water so I could pull up my swimsuit.

I guess I should have enjoyed the fun of acting like a mermaid. However, mermaids are always pictured with long flowing hair to cover up their breasts. My hair was in a swim cap, not available for the cover up job. Come to think of it, in all the pictures of mermaids I have seen, their hair is always dry and wavy, perfect for the cover-up job. Wet, stringy hair would not work nearly as well. Of course all the people on the beach enjoyed the whole show. It isn't every day one could see a naked lady. I did get a few catcalls and whistles when I returned to the beach for our picnic. Just mark it up to one of life's little adventures.

PAYBACK TIME

In general, l don't care much for zoos. I don't like to see animals that are used to wide open spaces, cooped up into confined cages. The exceptions are the wild animal parks where the animals are given acres of land to roam and enjoy doing all the things animals like to do. I remember a scene in the movie, "Planet of the Apes." Human space travelers come upon a planet inhabited by apes with advanced intelligent way of life. It was the human visitors who ended up in cages for the apes to study with curiosity.

As far as zoos go, the zoo in San Diego was, for the most part, designed to give the animals a reasonable amount of space. However, l can remember a couple of times when the frustration of confinement led to some amusing tricks of payback time. In one large cage was a magnificent male silverback gorilla. He would sit quietly watching as a crowd of spectators gathered in front of his cage. When he determined that the crowd was large enough, he would start to dance around, much to the delight of the people watching. Then suddenly he would stop pickup a handful of poop and, with uncanny accuracy, fling the mess through the bars of the cage hitting the unsuspecting people. As the crowd widely scrambled to get out of range, the delighted gorilla danced up and down hooting with joy. We saw this scenario played out several times.

In another part of the zoo was an elephant exhibit. It was designed with a large concrete covered area where the elephants could move about. This was separated from the visitors by a fairly narrow, dry moat some fifteen feet deep. It was one of our favorite spots to hang out for one of the elephants had made up her own little game. She would watch and wait for a family to come up close to the moat fence. I swear she had a knack of picking out a well dressed group. Then, as they stood there watching her, she would nonchalantly amble over to her watering trough, dip her trunk into the water to get a trunk full, then walk back over with her trunk held in a curve and get as close as possible to the unsuspecting visitors and fling out her trunk to spray them full in the face. Of course, most people laughed it off as a good joke on them.

One other story comes to mind about animals turning the tables on us humans. Several years ago l saw a TV special about a sanctuary for the endangered orangutans. Julia Roberts was the visitor to the area. In one sequence she was walking down a trail and a large dominant male orangutan jumped down from a tree to meet her. He looked her over and probably decided she would make a good addition to his harem. With cameras rolling, he started to carry her away with his long arms around her. At this point, the cameramen decided to stop the filming. It was all they could do to rescue her and prevent the ape from carrying her off. They didn't say how they managed to save her, perhaps by the use of a tranquilizing gun.

I am sure there are many stories such as these, where our animal friends decide to have a little fun at our expense. I, for one, applaud their cleverness. It is fun to know we aren't the only creatures with a sense of humor.

THE LURE OF GOLD

It was in the late 1950's; our two boys were not yet teenagers. Their dad was an avid fisherman and was dedicated to teaching his sons all about the techniques and delights of fishing. Our favorite, and in fact only favorite, vacations were trips to camp by streams or rivers where fish could be caught. In the planning for our vacations the one and only requirement of where we would go was that the fishing had to be good. Often this meant we would travel beyond the more popular campgrounds into uninhabited wilderness locations.

On one of these vacations, it was decided we would camp out by the Mad River, which is situated in the mountainous regions of northern California. We set up our camp in a lovely grove of pines, pleased to find we were, indeed, quite alone. To make matters even better, there were lots of fish eager to be caught! We all decided this was going to be a really fine vacation. However, on awakening the first morning we detected the sound of a motor. It seemed to be coming from a short distance downriver. Upon investigating we were amazed to discover a full scale river dredging operation in progress. There were four big burly men busy at work. There was a large generator hooked up to a wide suction hose. One man, in scuba gear, was directing the hose under water on the bottom of the riverbed. At the other end the hose was disgorging gravel and small rocks into a long wooden trough set up by the riverbank. There the other men were sorting through the gravel as it tumbled along the trough. They were not very happy to see us come by. But, I guess, they determined we were not any kind of threat, because they soon began to tell us what they were doing. They were looking for gold flakes and nuggets which could be found in the pockets and hollows of the riverbed. The gold, being heavier than sand and gravel, would settle there as it was being washed downstream. When we asked them if they were having any success, they showed us a glass vial of gold flakes they had found so far that day. It appeared to be about two ounces. At that time gold was worth about $350 per ounce. Not too bad for a couple hours of work. I don't know if their operation was being done legally with a permit, etc. We didn't ask!

We later came onto their camp located back among the trees. They had hauled in a small camping trailer. There was a huge, ferocious dog on a long chain guarding the camp. He barked loudly when he saw us nearby. I am sure any gold stored there would be perfectly safe from any intruders.

With all that was going on, we decided to move to another camping area where the fishing would be a little more peaceful. But I can't help but wonder how much gold those men were able to find. At the price of gold today, $1,600 per ounce, I am sure every flake and nugget has been taken from that river.

THE TREE HOUSE

We had moved into a neighborhood ideal for two adolescent boys. The house was on a street with little traffic. Across the street was a parcel of undeveloped land, which fell away into a small brush filled canyon. It was a perfect place for countless hours of exploration or "cowboys and Indians". At the rear of our house we had a fine shady back yard, but best of all, there was another yard behind where a small citrus tree orchard had been planted. We called this area "the back, back yard". It was hidden from view by a low vine covered wall and it was decided, the place our two boys, Gary and Dave, could call their own to do whatever they fancied.

This back, back yard became the site of numerous projects, from building rickety go carts (that fell apart on trial runs) to the ambitious plan of digging an underground room. The problem with that idea was the hardpan soil. After months of ardent shovel work, the boys managed to dig down only deep enough to sit down in their excavation without bumping their heads on the roof they had made from boards and palm branches. For their next project Gary and Dave decided to build a tree house. In addition to the small grapefruit, lemon and orange trees, there was one other tree in the back, back yard. It was very much on the scrawny side. The trunk was not much over eight inches in diameter, but it did fork out into three or four branches about six feet above the ground. In the judgment of the two boys this had real possibilities for a grand tree house. They already had the ideal material for the flooring. They removed the plywood roof from the not too successful underground fort and, with a few hammered in nails, managed to secure it up in the forked branches of the tree. Now this was really "cool". There they were way up in the air surveying their domain, just like Tarzan of old. Nothing would do except try this splendid tree loft as a place to spend many summer nights. Their dad and I decided it was safe enough with our faithful dog, Gypsy, standing guard in her close by doghouse. So excited preparations were made. In the early afternoon sleeping bags were laid out on the plywood floor. The boys were eagerly waiting for night to arrive.

As soon as it became dark they were off on their adventure with a substantial snack in hand to ward off starvation. As it turned out, there was only one serious problem. The floor of the tree house was not only a little small for two sleeping bags, but it also was not level. Due to the available branches for support, the floor tilted at a rather severe angle. The wonderful plan to spend the first of many nights in their tree house only lasted for three or four hours. For, even before their parents headed for bed, there was a little knock at the back door. The two adventurers had had enough! The thought of their comfortable, level beds was too strong to resist.

The tree house did survive for a few more months as a daytime perch, but it never developed any walls and was never used as a little boy's overnight lair!

THE MARBLE RUN

My maiden name is Brush. My father's line goes back to England. In the early 1600s two brothers from the Brush clan immigrated to America and set up adjacent farms on Long Island. The occupation of farming passed down through the generations for my father was born into a farmer family in the late 1800s.

I don't know how far back the tradition of a marble run goes in the family history, but my dad told of having one to play with when he visited his grandparents. And, as a child he and his siblings had one to play with in their home.

First let me explain what a marble run is. It is made of wood and stands about three feet high. At the top is a shallow basin to receive a handful of marbles. From there the marbles run down on a slant with a series of long pieces of wood scooped out so the marbles won't fall out of the trough. These wood strips are about two feet in length and zigzag back and forth at least ten times before going into a container at the end of the run. There is a rounded cup at each turn to guide the marbles around the corner into the next run. It is a game that seems to fascinate small children. As children we spent hours watching the marbles race down the track; the heavier the marble the faster it ran. Of course, it was always fun to take the box at the bottom of the run away and watch the marbles run all over the floor.

At the birth of my first child my parents were away in India as missionaries but when I was pregnant again three and a half years later they had just retired and returned to America. When I was about eight months pregnant they came to stay with us so that mother could help out when the baby arrived. Our older child, Gary, was three and a half and in the middle of potty training. Part of the routine was to take him to the toilet every half hour or so to make sure he didn't wet his pants; mother took over that duty. One day Gary having been dragged away from some game announced to his grandma, "I will be sure be glad when you go home"; she took it all in good humor.

Meanwhile as dad was at a bit of a loss for something to do he decided he would make a marble run for the children. Now my first husband, Pete, was no mechanic. He hardly knew which end of a screwdriver to use, so dad had few tools at his disposal. He bought some two by two strips of wood. He hand chiseled out the trough for the marbles. He asked me to save soup cans so that he could make the rounded curves for the turns. It was a true labor of love. Gary was delighted with the whole result and as the new baby, Dave, grew older he also loved to play with the marble run.

That same marble run is now sixty-two years old. It has had to undergo a few repairs through the years but is still bringing pleasure to young children. It was there for Dave's children and is now in Dave's house among the toys and games for his grandchildren. How proud my dad would be to know his labor of love has brought so much fun to generations of his decedents.

— Years 40 & Beyond —

MOTORCYCLE ADVENTURES

When I first met Fred we were in our late thirties. I was a widow with two teenage sons. When we started dating we found an opportunity to broaden our experiences. I introduced Fred to parenting, camping and world travel. In return he introduced me to skiing and motorcycling. Fred owned a Honda 90. It was a very small motorcycle, only able to carry one person. It wasn't long before he tried to persuade me to give it a try. The whole idea did not appeal to me in the least. I had no desire to risk my life on such an unpredictable machine. But one afternoon he took me out to where there was a dirt road, which climbed up a small hill. We took the motorcycle out of the car and he demonstrated several times how easy it all was to roar up and down the hill. I finally gave in, thinking it would serve him right if I ended up in a disaster! As I drove away up the hill I discovered it wasn't so bad after all, in fact it was sort of fun! I returned with a big grin on my face.

After we were married, Fred bought himself a larger machine, a Suzuki 250. We traded in the Honda 90 for a Honda 100, which had better springs and mobility. We took the bikes on many of our camping trips and had good times exploring back roads and trails. However, when the trails became steep and rocky I was not too happy or relaxed. On one excursion my front wheel hit a large rock. The bike stopped short and I went headfirst over the handlebars on to the trail. My face hit the rearview mirror and cut my upper lip. Not to worry! When we returned to camp Fred, being a doctor, had his emergency kit along and with a little anesthetic, sewed up my torn lip. Another time while taking a curve on a loose gravelly road, I fell off the motorcycle and smashed into a rocky cliff face. We discovered a large chunk was chipped out of the helmet I was wearing. Another close call. On another trip in southern Utah, we were exploring some back roads in the area. We stopped to look at our maps. Fred started off ahead and I was swarmed by a mass of biting horseflies. They were so vicious they took chunks of meat as they bit you. In my panic I flooded the motorcycle engine and couldn't get the thing started. I was in tears as Fred came back to see why I had not followed him. We did get the darned motorcycle started and got away from the monsters.

But other than that, I have to admit we did have lots of good times on our motorcycles. We found many lovely places we wouldn't have discovered without them. But when the time came, due to advancing years, we had to give them up. I do have to admit I didn't mourn their passing. But I am glad I had the courage to take that first ride because it opened up a whole new world of fun and adventure.

THE FIRST
BACKPACK ADVENTURE

When Fred and l first met he had never been camping. But it didn't take him long to develop a real love for the whole camping scene. We even spent part of our honeymoon on a tent camp out in the Sierra Nevada Mountains. However, the idea of backpacking, where you carry all your supplies on your back, was something new to both of us. My friend, Peggy (a co-teacher in my department at school) and her husband, tom, had done a lot of backpacking. They persuaded us to give it a try. They helped us borrow suitable packs, a tent and purchase food supplies. The four of us, with all our gear, drove from San Diego up to Palm Springs. This is a beautiful town, situated in the inland desert of Southern California. The two to three thousand foot San Jacinto Mountains stand hovering over the town on the west. These beautiful pine forested peaks were our destination. We planned to spend two or three days exploring that mountain wilderness.

It was about noon when we climbed aboard the cable car and were carried up to the mountaintop. We stopped by the ranger station to get trail maps and a camping permit. It was about that time, as we started off on the trail that the bad weather moved in from the west. Within less than half an hour, the rain had turned to snow. But that wasn't the worst of our problems. Apparently these mountains had been getting a great deal of recent rain and snow. As we came upon the designated campsites, we discovered the ground where the tents had to be set up, was covered by several inches of water! Our spirits matched the gloomy, soggy world around us.

It seemed the only sensible thing to do was to head back down on the cable car to the sunny, warm desert below. We knew of a good campground in Joshua tree National Park located about thirty miles from Palm Springs. By then it was late afternoon. By the time we had spent descending in the cable car, loading up our car and driving, it was eight or nine o'clock before we reached the campground at Joshua tree National Park. The other campers were all settled in. We were hungry and exhausted. We had to use the car's headlights to illuminate the process of setting up our backpack tents. The final blow was to discover (unlike the mountain forest camps) there was no water available to hydrate our lightweight, dehydrated food. We had to go around the other nearby campers to ask for any water they could spare. We cut our trip short to return home the next morning.

You would think that miserable introduction to backpacking would make us gladly give up the whole idea. But not so! Fred and I continued to develop our skills and outfitted ourselves with good equipment. We spent many wonderful days on numerous excursions into fabulous unspoiled wilderness. These adventures are some of our most treasured memories. It is good that we didn't give up after that first miserable experience.

A DANGEROUS GAME

One of our last backpacking trips was one I will never forget. Fred and I had been backpacking for several years. The delight of hiking just a few miles away from the throngs of people and finding a place to call our own, was what we enjoyed most of all. Most people think of Arizona as a dry desert. But the northern one-third is a high plateau with an elevation of 5,000 feet. There you can find pine forests with lakes and sparkling streams. One of these mountain streams is in the famous Oak Creek Canyon where the stream tumbles down towards the desert, just north of the beautiful town of Sedona. It is a very popular tourist camping area. We happened to talk to a ranger who told us about another canyon to the west which was just as beautiful, but had no roads. The only way to reach it was by backpacking. We could hardly wait to plan a trip there.

The next spring, during the Easter vacation, we drove from our home in San Diego. We planned to backpack into the canyon and spend 3 or 4 days exploring. We arrived on a Sunday and discovered the ranger station was closed. The question we had was whether we would find water in the canyon. However, we were in luck, for at a gas station we found a group of teenage boys. They assured us that a year round stream flowed through the canyon and it was one of their favorite places to fish. We did notice they drove off laughing, but figured they were just in high spirits.

This was very important information to know. The trail down into the canyon was over ten miles long. A gallon of water weighs 8.34 pounds. Our packs were already heavy, as we planned to stay several days. We were relieved to know we would find water, so we only filled a couple of quarts to drink on our way down. It was, by then, early afternoon. We found the trailhead and loaded up our packs. All went well and we reached the bottom of the canyon as the sun was setting. To our disappointment, the streambed was bone dry. There was no flowing water, or even a single pool. Those teenagers had played a trick on us! But it was no laughing matter; we had drunk our only water. There was only one thing to do. We needed to get out of there as soon as possible as night was falling. We climbed back up the trail as far as we could go before it became too dark to find our way. We set up a "dry" camp. Our dehydrated food was not an option without water. We ate some bread and crackers to satisfy our hunger. After a restless night we got up at dawn to finish the hike to our car. We never returned to that canyon again. We had learned a serious lesson—get the true story from a reliable source. Never trust a bunch of flaky kids. I am sure they never thought of how their false information endangered our lives.

THE CURIOUS BEAR

One summer Fred and 1 decided we would like to explore the area in the upper Yosemite Valley. We were, by now, quite seasoned backpackers. In order to have a true wilderness experience it was necessary to get away from the crowded campgrounds. We first went to the ranger station to get information about the trails, etc. We were informed that there was a bit of a "bear problem" in the backcountry. Many of the hikers had encountered bears in camp. We were advised, before going to sleep, to place everything to do with food (or even toothpaste) in a rucksack and suspend it from a tree branch at least twelve to fifteen feet above the ground. Fred, with some concern, asked if we met a bear would it be wise to bang loudly with a couple of tin plates. The ranger replied, "oh, no, that wouldn't scare it off, they are used to that." So it was, with some trepidation, we started off down the trail into the domain of the bear's country. Our intention was to hike in some twelve miles to an established backpack's camp, but we soon ran into a problem. I had failed to "double sock" my feet and consequently developed a large nasty blister on my heel. We had hiked about half way when we decided to stop and set up camp for the night. We found a large flat rock to use as our food preparation site and put up our tent nearby. After enjoying a pleasant afternoon and early evening, we carefully followed the ranger's advice regarding the supplies that had any odor that might attract bears.

I must admit that, as we settled down in our little pup tent for the night, we were quite apprehensive. I finally dropped off to sleep but Fred was not so lucky. He lay there listening for any unusual sounds. Then it happened! There, right by our flimsy little tent, not five feet away, he hears a bear rooting around our pots and pans with claws making noise on the rocky surface. Fred leaped out of our sleeping bag with a gigantic roar. I was sound asleep and with this wild explosion startled awake, thought for sure that a bear was in the tent with us! It did do the trick. The bear high tailed off into the forest. However, neither of us did much sleeping for the remainder of the night. We saw no more sign of the bear, but hiked out the next day deciding that backpacking in bear country was really not our thing.

MEXICO—OUR NEXT DOOR NEIGHBOR

I moved to San Diego in 1948. I was 20 years old and had just married an American Air force Officer I had met in India during WWII. My parents were missionaries there. I was delighted with the balmy climate after having spent 3 years in Pennsylvania; also it was great to have the beaches close by. We loved the outdoors and spent many weekends camping in the nearby mountains and desert. However, it was not long before we discovered the delights of Mexico, a few short miles to the South. The coastline of the Baja peninsula is made up of rocky cliffs, quiet secluded sandy coves and long stretches of uncrowded sandy beaches. Unlike the beaches around San Diego, we could spend a weekend along the coast of Baja and never share the view with another human being. The rocky shore had abalone and lobster within easy reach. But that was not all that Mexico had to offer. The peninsula has a ridge of mountains running down through the center. With an elevation of 3 to 5 thousand feet, these mountains are covered with pine forests and small lakes. One of our favorite spots was called Laguna Hansen. There one could camp out and swim in the cool lake without any other campers around. However, with our last trips there, the Mexican families had also discovered the area. They arrived with squealing kids and loud boom boxes to shatter the tranquility. The third area we discovered was on the eastern escarpment of the Baja Mountains. Where high cliffs towered over the dry desert, mountain streams tumbled over waterfalls and pools to empty onto the desert and form a shallow lake. This area was called Laguna Salada. Tucked up against the cliffs was a hot springs pool the water was a perfect temperature to spend hours of relaxation; again, with no other visitors. On one of our hikes in the nearby canyons, we discovered an ancient cave with pictogliphs on the walls. Perhaps we were the first to find this treasure.

We took many delightful trips to these three places we had discovered, often with friends and family. But then Mexico began to change. By the middle of the 1980s we began to hear stories about harassment of Americans camping on the beaches. The Mexican economy was in decline. Corruption was even more prevalent, (we had always been able to bribe an official who arraigned us with trumped-up charges). But now, it seemed the population was resentful of the rich Americans who flashed their money around. We heard the story of a group of Americans camping on a beach. Some off-duty soldiers came into camp and at gunpoint demanded all their money. They returned a few hours later to take everything of value the Americans had on hand. We also had a run-in with a group of off duty soldiers. We were camping on the beach. We had an inflatable dingy with us. Our friends, Bob and Joan, were retired and living full time on their yacht. They were anchored off shore from where we were, some 500 yards away. Two Mexican soldiers saw an opportunity to hassle Bob and Joan. They spoke no English, but wanted us to lend them our dingy to go out to the yacht. We pretended we couldn't understand their request. They finally left in disgust. Later that day, as we returned to camp, we found our 5 gallon gas tank was missing from the bed of our pickup truck. The two soldiers did finally find a way to get on our friend's yacht. They demanded to see whatever was on board and confiscated a revolver and a fishing pole. Some other friends of ours had a truck in Mexico impounded with the accusation that it had illegal drugs behind the seat. Of course, they had been planted there. The truck was returned after payment of several hundred dollars. All of this was enough for us to stop our trips into Mexico. Today the situation is even worse. With corrupt politicians and drug cartels, the tourist industry is in shambles. But for almost 40 years, we considered Mexico our own special place for fun and adventure. Perhaps someday it will be that way again!

A MOMENT OF MAGIC

During our travels one of the most interesting trips we took was a train ride across northern Mexico. We boarded the train in Chihuahua, then traveled west over the rugged Sierra Madre Mountains. The tracks wind through deep gorges parallel to the great Copper Canyon. This canyon is said to be larger than the Grand Canyon. When the Mexican government decided to build this railroad line in the 1920's the engineers from the USA said it could not be done so the Mexicans hired Swiss engineers to take on the project. The result is a spectacular journey through numerous tunnels, high spider web like trestles and cliff hugging tracks.

The train ride to the town of Topolabampo took three days. We traveled only during daylight hours, stopping at a different hotel every night. We were told this was to allow us to not miss any of the spectacular scenery. However, as l think back over the trip, I suspect it was more likely it was more prudent to run the train during the daylight hours so as to look out for any hazards along the tracks.

To go into this part of Mexico is like taking a trip back in time. The inhabitants of this remote mountain region are living just as they had for thousands of years untouched by any modern influences. They are the Tarahamora Indians who lived in small family groups in the caves scattered throughout the enormous canyon walls. They survived by tending small plots of land raising mostly corn and beans. The total canyon system is more than 5,000 feet deep and covered by abundant vegetation due to consistent rainfall.

At the time of our visit in the 1970's, the Indian population was still living mostly in their traditional cave homes. However, some have moved into towns, which developed around the tourist hotels. They were also learning to take advantage of the tourist money by selling their handmade baskets and fabrics at every train depot. The women still wore their colorful traditional handmade garments and jewelry.

We were able to visit with one of the Tarahamora families in their cave home. No furniture of any kind, only a fire pit for cooking. A real step back in time! One of the customs that seemed unusual was the selection of a mate. The Tarahamoras gathered together two or three times a year to celebrate and socialize. It was also an opportunity to meet prospective mates. The boys had many contests and games to show off their attributes to the young women. It was up to the girl to show her interest in a particular man. This was done by discreetly tossing a pebble to hit the man of her choosing. If he was not attracted to the pebble thrower, he would pretend to not have noticed. However, if all were agreeable, he would get up and chase the girl off into the surrounding woods. There they would consummate their mutual attraction and that established them as husband and wife. All pretty simple and straightforward!

Even though this entire trip is one of my most interesting adventures, there is one incident that made it an extra special memory. On this particular day we had debarked from the train quite early in the afternoon. Our group had taken a short walk along the canyon rim to enjoy the view of endless vistas of deep gorges and cliffs. I wandered away by myself and sat down on a rock to spend some quiet time. As l sat there l saw a beautiful large Mexican gray wolf emerge from some nearby trees. He was larger than a coyote, but not as large as the wolves in the northern USA. I think, at first, he didn't see me and proceeded to cross the meadow towards me. When he got within about twenty feet from where I sat he became aware of my presence. He stopped and calmly looked at me with his big yellow eyes. There was no fear, no aggression, and only curious consideration. For me, it was a truly magical moment. He stood there quietly studying me for two or three minutes, then unhurriedly turned and trotted away. It was such a precious experience for me. The Mexican grey wolf is, at present, considered the most endangered of all predators in North America. They estimate there are fewer than forty wild Mexican grey wolves in the USA. I feel that encounter was a very special privilege for me.

I am sure that, by now, the modern world with all of its influences has overwhelmed those simple Tarahamoras and their ancient way of life. I am so grateful to have had a glimpse into the way life was for the human race thousands of years ago.

MY VISIT TO THE TAJ MAHAL

There was a program on TV the other day giving the history of the Taj Mahal. It brought back the memory of my trip there during the 1980's. The tour was organized by my brother, Stan, who was a college professor and taught a course in Indian history. He had a contract with Air India airlines to set up tours during the summer months.

Our group was made up of twelve people: Stan and his wife, Bev, and me and my husband, Fred, another couple, friends of ours, and an assortment of Stan's students and a few students from other colleges. We spent three weeks touring interesting sites, including three trips up into the highlands of the Himalayas and a flight around Mount Everest. It was a fabulous three weeks.

Both Stan and I had been born and raised in India as children of American missionaries. I had taken a trip to see the Taj Mahal when I was a year old. I have a picture of our family with the Taj in the background, but of course I have no memory of that visit.

India has a most interesting ancient history. The first humans to arrive were from the migrations out of Africa some eighty thousand years ago. Another migration occurred when the Huns from central Europe moved down into the subcontinent, some six thousand years ago. They brought with them the beginning of the Hindu religion. Then in the twelfth century AD the Mongol warriors led by Genghis Khan, invaded and conquered northern India. They brought with them the new religion of Islam. There was a tolerance of the religion of Hinduism and the whole country prospered under the Mongol rule. The exotic spices and silks of India were in great demand in Europe which developed a well established trade.

By the early sixteen hundreds a new ruler took over the Mongol throne. His name was Shah Jahan. As was the custom he was married in his early teens to a child bride named Taj Mahal. It seems that they had a real love for each other, even though he had, later on, a vast harem of other wives and concubines.

In the 1630's Taj Mahal died giving birth to her fourteenth child. Shah Jahan was heartbroken and vowed to build the most beautiful mausoleum in her memory. He employed hundreds of artisans and builders to erect a tomb out of the most prized white marble available. It took the workers eight years to erect the most beautiful building ever built by man. It almost bankrupted the country in the process. Shah Jahan ruled for another thirty years. Then his son, by Taj Mahal, took over the throne and threw his father into prison for the rest of his life. From his prison cell he could look out and see the Taj Mahal in the far distance. Shah Jahan had plans to build an identical copy of the Taj Mahal in black marble across the river from the Taj, but ran out of money to do so. When he died his remains were placed in the Taj Mahal beside those of his beloved wife.

Throughout my life I had seen many picture of the Taj Mahal, but I was in for a surprise. Pictures do not do justice to the grandeur and size of the building. From the entrance gate the visitors look like ants as they enter the mausoleum. When we arrived for our visit the sun was setting; the beautiful white marble glowed with a soft pink light as if it came from within the stone. However, the beauty of the place does not end with the distant view, for as you enter the building you are enthralled by the exquisite inlay of semiprecious stones in patterns of flowers and vines decorating the walls of gleaming white marble. I was so delighted with the beautiful inlay that I purchased some examples of the work on decorative white marble plates. They were done by the descendants of the original artisans who worked on the Taj Mahal some three hundred fifty years ago. I still have them and would be happy to show them to you at anytime.

The actual tombs are located in a chamber below ground level. More mosaics decorate the walls there. We returned to visit the Taj by the light of a full moon. The entire building seemed to be floating in a glowing white light. This was one of my most rewarding experiences.

Although we observed the presence of policemen on our visit, today there is serious concern that radical terrorists will try to destroy this priceless work of art. There are extensive security regulations on visitors. My hope is for it to stand for centuries to come for it is one of the true wonders of the world.

RUBIES, THE GEM OF LEGENDS

It all started when I was planning a visit to Pakistan. The trip was organized and led by my brother, Stanley. Having spent my childhood in India, during the days before the breakup of India into two nations, I was eager to observe the changes that had taken place.

Our itinerary included a visit to an area where rubies were being mined, with an opportunity to purchase gems at a low price. It seemed to be a perfect time to buy a variety of rubies for rings, tietacs and earrings for family and friends.

Our tour guide took us to a reputable ruby merchant. I was thrilled to find a lovely selection of gems. I had brought along about three hundred dollars to purchase stones that I wanted that could be set later into Jewelry. I bought a total of about ten stones, each a caret or more in size.

Upon my return to the United States I was curious to see what the Jewelers would say about my purchases. The first store I tried the question I was asked was how much they had cost. With my answer, the immediate reply was that they were not real stones, only synthetics. After a couple of those reactions, I decided to not tell what I had spent. Whereupon the Jeweler was willing to examine the gems and stated they were, indeed, the genuine thing. I was told that synthetic and real rubies are actually almost identical when examined. The only discernible difference is that genuine rubies have slight imperfections.

In the next few months I had the rubies made into Jewelry for my family. My son, Gary, was living in Texas. Just before Christmas I made up a package for him and his wife, Mary. In it I included a ring made with a large ruby for Gary and a lovely set of earrings for Mary. My plan was to take them to the post office on my way to work. However, upon reaching the post office I discovered the package was not on the car seat. I recalled putting it on the top of the car before opening the door! With sinking heart, I retraced my route with no success. I returned to the post office to inform them of my error.

That afternoon, after work, I returned to the post office, just hoping for the remote possibility that the package had turned up. Much to my complete amazement it had! Someone had seen it on the side of the road, saw that it was ready for mailing and brought it to the post office. She did not leave her name so I could never thank her for her honest act. But I will always remember that there are many good and honest people in this world and I was fortunate to have such a person come into my life.

ARE YOU SPEAKING ENGLISH?

After completing college and earning his teaching credentials, our son Gary was looking for his first job as a teacher. A recruiter from Australia interviewed him. It seemed that there was a shortage of teachers there during the late 1970's. He signed a contract for three years. His assignment was to a small town called

Numurka, located about a hundred miles north of Melbourne.

As Australia was one place I had always wanted to visit, my husband, Fred, and I decided it would be an ideal time to go there while Gary was fulfilling his assignment. Our itinerary included first two weeks touring New Zealand, two more weeks in Australia and four days for a stopover in Tahiti on our way home to San Diego.

After a long flight, we landed in Auckland, a city on the north island of New Zealand. We were dropped off at a hotel for a few hours of rest. As we checked in at the front desk, we were amazed to discover we couldn't understand what the nice, helpful desk clerk was saying. Of course we knew and expected some different accent, but what we were hearing was like a totally different language. We finally managed to conduct our business with the clerk slowing down and using some hand gestures. It didn't take us too long to catch on to the New Zealand accent. We were able to communicate fairly well on our adventure driving a rented car on the north and south islands of New Zealand. It was a wonderful trip, full of fascinating sights and interesting encounters, and a subject for another time.

Upon our arrival in Australia, we were met by Gary and driven to the small town where he was teaching in the high school. We stayed there for about a week. It was interesting to discover the customs and protocol quite different from back home. Activities were divided into those appropriate for men and not to be open for women. Sports programs are not associated with the schools but rather organized by the entire town. It was Australian football season. We attended a game between Numurka and a neighboring town. It was the women's job to organize a big potluck dinner for everyone. The competing teams were made up of men, young and old, from the town's residents. The stands were overflowing with wildly enthusiastic fans. During team huddles, flocks of men would run out onto the field to hear the strategy plans. However, no women could step onto the field, it would bring bad luck! The same held true at half-time. Men crowded into the locker room to encourage their home team. The game of Aussie football is rough and violent. Gary was playing on the team. During one of the plays he was flattened by an opposing player and failed to get up. Much to my distress, the game went on with him still lying on the field. I was sitting next to the coach of the team. Upon my frantic inquiry, he assured me all would be fine. And sure enough, in a couple of minutes Gary did get up and joined in the play.

Another rule of protocol is that no respectable woman goes into a bar. During our visit, Gary took us to dinner at one of his favorite restaurants. He and Fred would go into the bar for happy hour. Seeing as I could not join them, Gary asked one of the waitresses to visit with me. She was from a ranch in the "outback" region of the country. Even though I was doing pretty well understanding the Aussie dialect, I was at a total loss when it came to her rural accent. Each evening as we visited together, I pretended to understand what she was telling me. I smiled and murmured encouraging comments without any idea of what she was saying. I am sure she thought I was a little dimwitted. Perhaps, with the advent of worldwide communication by television, etc., the world will become less diverse. It seems that English will become the universal language in the years to come. But it may take a long time before we all speak English with the same dialect. That would be a shame. The world would not be as interesting a place to visit, with everyone speaking in exactly the same way.

BEAUTIFUL TAHITI

It was on our return trip from a visit to Australia that my husband, Fred, and I planned a stopover on the Polynesian Island of Tahiti. We had made arrangements with another couple to meet there for a stay of five or six days. Our plane first landed on the main island at the town of Papeete, which is the only large city in the island group these islands are volcanic in origin. Each one is a tropical, tree covered, craggy peak surrounded by white sand beaches and amazingly clean, sparkling, turquoise blue waters.

We stayed a couple of days in Papeete, a fascinating city of laid back South Seas laziness, combined with Western bustle and activity. The outdoor market filled with exotic tropical fruits, seashells, fish and other unusual items, was a delight.

One incident stands out in my memory. Tahiti was originally a French colony. We were exploring the boat harbor and l needed to use the restroom facilities. I discovered a most interesting toilet. In the center of the bowl was a funny looking nozzle: I bent over the bowl to see how it worked. When I pressed the lever a jet stream of water shot up hitting me full in the face and soaking my hair. I screamed in surprise. After attempting to dry myself off I joined up with the others; I took a lot of teasing. It seems l had encountered the famed French style toilet called a "bidet".

However, the true highlight of our trip was to the island of Bora-Bora. This is the island jewel, the setting for many movies. Not only does it have a rugged volcanic mountain center surrounded by wide white coral sand beaches, but in addition a barrier reef encircling the whole island. This creates a lagoon of crystal clear blue water as warm and calm as to appear transparent. Our accommodations were widely spaced thatched roof cottages under swaying coconut palms. One had to be alert when walking as the coconuts might drop from above at any moment. With a fall of some twenty feet, a person could be knocked out cold if hit by one. We had been advised to bring along some cans of whole corn to feed the fish. It was wonderful to spend hours snorkeling in the warm water of the lagoon. We took Ziploc bags tucked in our swimsuits to feed the marvelous variety of colorful fish. As soon as we scattered the corn they would come in schools to eat right out of our fingers. A truly delightful experience.

With few other tourists, friendly native islanders and gorgeous scenery, our trip to Tahiti and Bora-Bora was an unforgettable experience.

OUR GARDEN OF EDEN

One of our favorite places to vacation was on Lake Powell. With the construction of Glen Canyon Dam the mighty Colorado River was backed up to form a lake some two hundred miles in length. What made it so special was the canyon country made accessible by the formation of the lake. Southern Utah is .a land of spectacular red rock sandstone canyons. We spent many vacations exploring the numerous side canyons where the lake water invited us to discover hidden wonders of narrow slots where the sculptured cliffs soared high overhead.

On one of these adventures we decided to find the arch formed in the sand-stone rock. It was located on the Escalante River, a tributary flowing into the lake from the north. We had rented a twelve foot boat with an outboard motor. Loaded with our camping gear Fred and I were accompanied by our special camping companion, Tawny, a German Shepherd mix, who "lived" for our outdoor adventures.

As soon as we left the lake and started motoring up the river we ran into some difficulty. It was late summer and the river flow became so shallow it was not possible to use the motor. Undeterred we jumped out of the boat and proceeded to wade through the shallow water pushing the boat along. We continued in this manner for about a half mile around a couple of bends until finally, we reached the spot where high above on the side of a towering canyon wall, we discovered the stone arch.

The whole vista was a place of enchantment. Below the red canyon wall the quiet river was lined with stately cottonwood trees. The river banks were covered with soft green grass, a perfect place to set up our campsite. Across from our spot another stream tumbled out of a narrow slot canyon to join the main river.

We spent three days in that enchanted place. It was as if we were the only humans on earth. The sun sparkled down on us. Our only visitors were the canyon Wrens and other birds that seemed happy to share their world with us. The nights were magical as well. There was a full moon and a sky crowded with countless glimmering stars. One night, after we were tucked away in our tent, a lone coyote wandered by. Even tawny didn't seem to mind his serenade to the moon.

On one of the days we explored up the slot canyon across from our camp. Tawny was our enthusiastic companion. In one place we had to scramble up a steep rock face, which was too steep for the dog. We solved the problem by making a sling with a jacket attached to a rope. Tawny seemed to understand the whole plan and hung motionless in this contraption as we hauled her up the cliff face, and back down on our return to camp.

When it was time to leave, on our way back to the main lake, we were able to float down the river with the motor tilted up, a much easier way to travel. But those days spent in that place will stay in my memory forever. No doubt, the shallow river kept other boaters away. But for us, we could imagine that, for a few days, we were Adam and Eve in a beautiful garden created just for us alone.

SKINNY DIPPING

I am not quite sure where this urge to swim without any clothes has come from. My dear mother, always a bit on the plump side, never learned to swim. In fact, the college she attended in Pennsylvania had a requirement that every student had to learn to swim in order to graduate. Although she gave it her earnest effort, the college had to waive the requirement in her case. Throughout the rest of her life she never owned a swimsuit. Our beach excursions found mother fully clothed sitting under a beach umbrella. However, on the other hand my oldest brother, John, loved to swim in the nude. He was a very proper and dignified college professor, the head of the geography department at Rutgers University. We all were a little amazed and amused by his propensity to fling off his clothes whenever the occasion allowed. On his trips to San Diego to visit us he always managed to fit in a day at "Black's Beach" in an isolated location along the coast. Although he invited us to join him, we always declined. I guess the sense of modesty prevailed.

However, if I am certain no one else is around, I have on occasion discovered the delight of skinny dipping. My first time was when I was a junior in high school. Our boarding school was located in the Himalayan Mountains of India. The dormitory for high school girls was about a mile from the main campus of the school. One morning my two best friends and I were walking up the trail to the school. It was one of those exceptionally beautiful days. The sun was bathing the world in a golden light that sparkled on every tree and bush. The air was crystal clear, as only mountain air can be. We decided it was just too beautiful a day to be indoors, especially in a classroom. Although it would mean we would be in trouble, we figured it would be worth it.

We knew of a secluded place where a little mountain stream made a waterfall with a small pool at the bottom. After reaching the spot we stripped down to our underclothes and spent the morning there. Like three water nymphs we splashed and played in the warm sun. Probably all the more fun because we were playing hooky! On our return to school that afternoon, I don't recall what punishment we received. Actually, throughout my life I only remember the punishments I had that I felt were undeserved.

Later on as an adult I have, on occasion, gone swimming without a swimsuit. Fred and I discovered that on our backpack trips it was possible to find a world devoid of other people just by hiking a few miles from paved roads. A perfect place to play at being Adam and Eve in the pools of a stream. But the best place of all to go skinny dipping is in the ocean. It may be due to the different feel of salt water or the way the waves wash over your skin. On our camping trips to the coast of Mexico we often set up our camp with no one else around. I remember one night's swimming in particular. The waves were sparkling with the bloom of phosphorescent microorganisms. Each breaking wave glowed with a shimmering light. As we splashed around in the water, cascades of luminescence flowed over our bodies, truly a unique experience.

One of the items on my bucket wish list is to swim again in an ocean full of luminescence. It might not be so wonderful in the cold waters of the Northwest, but perhaps I could find myself on a secluded southern beach under a full moon, just one more time.

AN ADVENTURE OF A LIFETIME

I don't know how it happened that we decided to go on a five day camping trip, on horseback, in the mountains of Wyoming. We thought up this idea with our good camping buddies, Bob and Nancy. The thing is none of us had ever done much riding on horseback. All four of us were well within the category of "tenderfoot". As we spread the word about our planned trip we were told by horse riding friends that we would have some real problems with sore bottoms and aching knees being bent outward from several hours in the saddle. The more experienced riders told us it would help if we dismounted every half hour or so and walked our horses for fifteen minutes. Then, for preventing sore backsides, I made four saddle pads from some thin dense foam covered with denim and ties to secure them on the hard saddles. As the time of the trip drew near, we felt a little more confident about our pending adventure.

We drove from San Diego to the ranch located in the Wind River Range, part of the Rocky Mountains, in a remote area of Wyoming close to the Continental Divide. Early morning of the first day we hauled our personal gear in duffel bags and our crafty little saddle pads out to the horse corral, where the cowboys were loading up the horses. At the sight of our saddle pads the cowboys had some difficulty keeping straight faces as they helped us tie the pads in place. We explained we were novice riders but that didn't seem to alter their amused reaction.

We set off for our five to six hour trail ride to the campsite some ten miles into the remote mountains. Our train of horses was led by our cowboy guide DJ, his wife, Jenny, who would be our cook, one other cowboy to help set up camp and the four of us greenhorns. In addition to three pack horses to carry all the supplies and gear, there was a rambunctious little Australian sheep dog named Terry. He immediately took over his role of making sure the whole horse train moved along together in perfect order. However his job was unexpectedly made more difficult when, after traveling along for a while, we four dismounted to continue with walking our horses. Little dog, Terry, was extremely upset. He barked at us to tell us we shouldn't do that. We definitely belonged on top of our horses; he never did accept our strange behavior.

By mid-afternoon we reached the campsite. It was a lovely spot among the trees at the edge of a grassy meadow. Our hosts got busy setting up camp. The tents were very different from any I had ever seen. They were made of heavy canvas, tepee shaped, with a rope attached to the point, which was thrown up over a tree branch to pull the tent up. The circular aides were then staked out to form a wigwam type shelter. The other supplies and food had been carried in panniers (a basket shaped to fit along a horse's sides). There were some panniers made of plastic, which held the perishable foods, these were settled down in the nearby icy stream to keep the food cold, a natural icebox. The horses were unsaddled and led out to the grassy meadow where each was tethered to a large log to prevent them straying too far.

There was only one serious problem with this idyllic setting: The presence of big hungry mosquitoes. As long as you stayed in the sun they let you alone, but if you ventured into the trees they were there and in full attack mode. This made it quite a challenge to answer the call of nature. With no toilet facilities this meant a trip into the trees. As soon as tender bottoms were exposed the swarms attached, making it necessary to be as speedy as possible. This was the only time, as a female, that the male anatomy seemed to have some real advantages.

As evening came we "tender-feet" were aware DJ and Jenny were watching us closely. Upon questioning they admitted they were quite impressed over our absence of being sore after a day of riding. They were used to seeing the guests being most uncomfortable from riding. In the meantime, Terry, the dog, took his duties seriously making sure everyone did their jobs. He checked on the horses and was on guard throughout the night to warn us of any bears, or such, which might wander into camp.

We had a great dinner cooked over the campfire, a pleasant evening telling stores around the fire and a good night's sleep. As we woke the next morning DJ discovered one of the horses was missing. He did some muttering under his breath and said he knew what had happened. That darned horse had gone back home to the ranch, dragging the log along with him. DJ saddled up and rode off to return by midday with the homesick horse. That horse was "double logged" from then on.

Our days were spent exploring the nearby flower filled meadows, fishing for crafty native trout in the crystal clear, sparkling brooks and discovering fabulous mountain vistas. We learned to help saddle the horses and became more comfortable in the saddle. One morning, as we were saddling up the horses, Jenny asked me if I would like to ride her horse for the day. I agreed and started to transfer my saddle pad over to the saddle on her horse. She stopped me and grudgingly admitted that what she wanted was to try out the saddle pad. After trying it for the day she said it felt really comfortable. She explained the macho culture of the cowboy world would never do anything to soften the ride on a hard saddle. She thought it was great for us to make riding easier.

After three days having a wonderful adventure we hated to see it was time to end our vacation. We broke camp and saddled up for our return to the ranch. Our little watchdog, Terry, had one more antic up his sleeve. About halfway home we came up onto a mountain top meadow. There, only fifty yards in front of us, was a huge herd of elk, some two hundred by count, moving across the meadow. We stopped in our tracks, thrilled to have the chance to observe such a unique sight. But not for long! It was just too much for Terry with his built in herding instinct. In spite of DJ's urgent commands, he tore off across the meadow causing the elk to scatter in opposite directions. It was total bedlam with little Terry in hot pursuit. When DJ finally got him back to us there wasn't a single elk in sight. The rest of the ride was completed without incident. Even though we never took another trip on horseback, I look back at that horse pack trip as one of the best vacations of my life.

A VISIT TO SHANGRI-LA

I was born and raised in India, my parents were American missionaries. My brother, Stan, as an adult, had spent several years in Pakistan as a university teacher. He later taught in a college in Connecticut. He spent his summers organizing tour groups to India and Pakistan under a contract with Air India.

In the early 1990s I joined him on one of these trips to Pakistan. Part of the itinerary was a bus trip into the high Himalaya Mountains of Northern Pakistan. The narrow, winding dirt road climbed up past the most southern snow covered peaks onto the plateau; an elevation of fifteen thousand feet. The bus ride was a hair-raising adventure. The road was only wide enough for one vehicle with occasional wider turnouts. If two vehicles met, one had to back up to the last wide spot. With no walls or fences, the view out the window of the sheer cliffs was not for the faint of heart. Gratefully, there was little traffic.

Our destination was the Hunza Valley. The inhabitants were decedents of the invading armies of the Huns during medieval times. Supposedly this was the same valley in Milton's novel "Paradise Lost", where the lost mountaineer came across Shangri-La, "where one never grows old". The way that myth got credence was due to the appearance of the inhabitants. They kept no birth records. Due to the rain shadow created by the over twenty thousand foot peaks to the south, no rain or snow ever reaches this plateau. The harsh, dry climate and outdoor lifestyle of the people, results in extremely aged and wrinkled skin. Early explorers, finding a wrinkled, weathered people still full of vigor and energy, concluded this was a place of eternal youth.

Those of us on the tour had some fun imagining that upon entering the area we had miraculously become young again, only to return to our true age with our departure. (I remember the movie "Paradise Lost", with Ronald Coleman, where the woman he has persuaded to leave the Valley with him, suddenly collapses and turns into an old, withered, hag.)

The history of the area is most interesting. The ancient Silk Road extending all the way from Europe and the Middle East to India and far off China passed through this valley. It was the chief occupation of the inhabitants to live off the payments they demanded for the caravans to pass through their land. With tall towers built near the road and window slots bristling with bows and arrows, the travelers had little choice but to pay up or be killed.

Their present way of living is also unique. They are now mostly an agricultural society, their main crop is apricot of such high quality they are in demand worldwide. Our visit was in October. The fruit had been picked and every flat rooftop was covered with golden apricots drying in the sun.

As the Valley is so arid, with only occasional traces of rain, the orchards are irrigated by a canal system built thousands of years ago, which brings water from distant glaciers and rivers.

These same houses, built centuries ago, are still maintained and lived in by the descendants of the family. They are very simple; made of stone and dirt mortar as no forests grow at such a high elevation). There is only one large room with a tire pit in the center and a hale above in the roof to let out the smoke. We were invited to visit the Ruler's home. His family is the fifteenth generation in the ruling line of ancestors. His dwelling was not much larger than the other houses, but he did have the addition of Persian rugs covering the dirt floors. He had also been educated in England, and so was the only one in the Valley who could speak English.

Our visit was such a unique opportunity to see a culture and way of life as lived for hundreds of years. For a moment, we could step back in time to a simpler way of living. So different from the complicated, hectic lives we live in modern society. It is only with a chance to see it, that we need to realize that for millions of people, this is still their way of life throughout the world. We tend to think our modern society is all there is.

SANTORINI

One of our overseas adventures was a cruise on the Mediterranean. The cruise started in Rome and traveled down the west coast of Italy to explore the ruins of Pompeii, truly a fascinating glimpse of an ancient city buried by a volcanic eruption in 79 AD. So sudden that the inhabitants were unable to flee, their bodies encased in ashes where they died.

We stopped at many sites along the shore to explore ruins of cities that prospered during the Roman Empire. Athens and Istanbul were especially interesting. However, our day spent on the island of Santorini was one of the highlights of the trip. It is an island in the eastern Mediterranean, a possession of Greece with a fascinating history. In prehistoric times there was an extraordinarily advanced civilization. At that time the large island was round with a volcano at its center with several towns along the shoreline.

Then in 1500 BC a series of earthquakes warned the inhabitants of a pending eruption. The people all evacuated before the volcano exploded. It was so violent that the whole mountain blew to bits. Where once the island stood, a massive abyss filled by the waters of the sea. All that remains of the former island is a high rim of a crescent shaped island called Santorini. A few other small islets remain of the caldera rim across water filled space of some 20 miles. This is all that is left of that prehistoric volcano.

It was several centuries before Santorini was re-inhabited. A layer of volcanic ash some 30 feet deep buried everything. However that ash makes good soil for agriculture. Today there are several small towns on the island. One of the main crops is grapes to make wine. Due to the scarcity of fresh water, each grape vine is trained to rest on the ground in a circle some four feet across to conserve moisture.

One of the prehistoric towns has been excavated to reveal the houses as they stood 3,500 years ago, truly an awesome experience to walk those streets and imagine the people who lived there so long ago.

The main town on Santorini is located high above the sea at the end of the island. When we disembarked from the ship's launch at the shore below, we had a choice of climbing a flight of 600 steps or taking an incline car up to the town. It is a charming little town, as all the houses were painted white. It's beautiful contrast to the azure blue sea.

We spent the morning visiting an interesting museum and shopping. When lunchtime arrived we decided we would like to try an authentic Greek restaurant, as the food on the ship was mostly American cuisine. We dropped by a small gift ship to inquire where we could find real Greek cooking. The owner, a nice, pleasant young man, told us of a fabulous place just down the block with the assurance that the food was authentic Greek. As we settled down at a table the waiter brought us a menu. We noticed immediately that he didn't have a Greek accent. In fact, his accent sounded very much like an American accent. Upon our inquiry, he admitted he had moved to Santorini from Brooklyn a few years ago. He and his brother had opened this restaurant and did all the cooking. (So much for authentic Greek cuisine!) Actually the food did taste very good. But we found out that the nice man in the shop up the street was their cousin and was diligently steering tourists to the family restaurant. We figured it was all part of the tourist scene.

Our cruise exploring the world of our past was a fascinating adventure. Our own American history is so short; it is valuable to see further back in time.

EXPLORING THE GILA RIVER

When we first met, my husband, Fred, had never been camping. Having grown up in Detroit, he was a real "city boy". I, on the other hand, had camped out all my life. However, it didn't take long for him to embrace the idea wholeheartedly.

He loved nature and was delighted to be in the great outdoors. In fact within a short time, some friends of ours introduced us to backpacking. The idea was that by carrying everything you would need on your back, you could go just a few short miles and find yourself in a place without any other people, a place to be at one with nature. We were in our middle forties, full of energy and roaring to go. However, that touch of city boy made Fred insist that we always brought a zip-up tent along. No creepy-crawlies would share our sleeping bags.

We learned by trial and error that the best time to backpack in the southwest was in spring, before the onset of the monsoon rains, which usually arrived in early July. We discovered it was not much fun to be hunkered down in a tiny tent trying to prepare dinner on a one burner stove with the rain coming down in torrents outside.

One spring we decided on a trip hiking up the Gila River in New Mexico. The source of the Gila is a lovely mountain lake high on the northern plateau. From there the river cascades down onto the southern plains. It would take about three days to hike up to the lake from where we started. We had been advised to watch out for snakes, especially rattlesnakes. We met a couple on our first day and they told us it was a good idea to sweep the ground ahead with our walking sticks when going through grassy meadows, as they had come across several rattlesnakes. We took their advice but didn't encounter any snakes.

However, on the second day of our hike we found a welcome sight. We discovered a side creek with a hot spring flowing into a small pool. Just a perfect place to relax and wash off the sweat and grime. We had seen no one all day, so stripped off our clothes and settled down into the warm water. As we were luxuriating in the delightful warm water, Fred happened to look over at a ledge close by. We were not the only ones enjoying the hot spring. There stretched out on the rock was a coral snake, the only one I have ever seen in the wild. It was definitely the real McCoy! There is another snake that mimics the coloring of a coral snake and is not poisonous. The saying goes "black on red, do not dread. Black on yellow, kill a fellow". That was the end of our bath! We leaped out of the water, threw on our clothes and beat a hasty, very undignified retreat.

On the remainder of our hike we did encounter a couple more rattlesnakes and gave them a wide berth. We were glad we had our little zip-up tent to sleep in. But other than the snakes, the trip was great. We came across a family of beavers. We sat quietly by to watch them at their work. They paid no attention to us. It was a real treat to share their world for a while.

In hindsight, I can understand why we had that Gila River hike mostly to ourselves. Perhaps it is best to leave that wilderness to our "friends", the snakes!

TO THE TOP OF MT. EVEREST

Our small, twelve passenger plane was wending its way through the mountain valleys of Nepal. Towering above us on both sides were the more than twenty thousand toot peaks of the Himalayan Mountains. In the valley below we could see the century's old terraced grain fields stacked up the mountain slopes.

We had left the city of Kathmandu, the capital of Nepal. A city of noisy congestion, filled with fascinating sights and sounds in addition to multiple Buddhist temples and shrines, street vendors hawking their wares, mountain people in their colorful clothes mixing with modern society with all its trappings.

We were on my first return trip to India, since my departure some thirty years ago. My brother, Stan, was our tour guide, as he had taken many previous trips to India and Pakistan. Our destination was the small mountain town of Pakora. A far outpost nestled up against the magnificence snow covered giants of the mountain range.

As we approached the tiny airport, the pilot of our plane circled the runway to warn of our landing. Whereupon, the cows that had been grazing there were herded off to the side so as to clear the runway. I use the term "runway" loosely, for in actuality it was not much longer than a city block. One end dropped off abruptly into a deep valley, it was a bit like landing on an aircraft carrier. Our pilot approached with reduced speed over the drop off, so that when he touched down he could come to a rapid stop before crashing into the mountainside ahead. It was with shaking knees we all climbed out of that little plane.

We spent a couple of glorious sun drenched days in that magic place seeing sunrises and sunsets that turned those magnificent towering peaks to gold was an experience never to be forgotten. But the main purpose for our stay in

Pakora was a flight to Mt. Everest, only a few miles away. For this excursion we flew in an even smaller six passenger plane. We took off the "aircraft carrier" sized runway where the plane dipped a little as it ran out of ground. Then we soared up through the mountain valleys until we saw ahead a massive pyramid shaped peak. This was the famous Everest, the highest mountain on earth at 29,035 feet. Actually, if we had not been told which one was Everest, we wouldn't have known it. The other mountains nearby are all well over 25,000 feet or more. It is just another of those giants. Our little plane seemed to be not much larger than a bird among those vast spaces.

We circled close to the mountain, but not close enough to see any climbers. Perhaps, the routes to the summit were on another side. I felt very fortunate to not be one of those climbers. It did seem to be a too wild and hostile place for tiny humans to exist. It is beyond my understanding why the call to climb such mountains is irresistible to so many.

The next day we left the region to continue our tour to other places in India. But our side trip into those magnificent mountains remains one of my most treasured memories.

A PLACE OF ENCHANTMENT

It was just by luck that we heard about it. We were staying in our RV in the campground at Zion National Park. We found ourselves drawn back time after time to that special wonderland in the Red Rock country of southern Utah. For anyone who has never had the experience of standing in the bottom of a narrow sandstone gorge with red cliffs towering one to two thousand feet above you it is difficult to explain the beauty of it all. The glow of sunlight on the red cliffs all around you fills the day with warm golden light, the thought of the millions of years it took to carve out this valley with wind, rain and the running water in the river at your feet. Fred and l found we were never bored with the prospect of exploring the trails and vistas of that place.

On one of our trips, as we were browsing in the visitor's center, we happened to overhear two park rangers talking about another close by canyon called "the

Great West Canyon". In answer to our questions we were told of a canyon, not accessible by road, that was a favorite destination of the rangers on their off- duty days. It was sort of their secret but they showed us a journal, which gave directions to get to this special undeveloped canyon. We had a small tape recorder so we recorded the directions to use later.

On our next trip to the area we came prepared for an adventure of a lifetime. We brought our backpacks and enough provisions for four or five days. Our sweet dog "Tawny" had her own saddlebags to carry her kibbles. We found the trail-head parking lot, secured the car and headed off down the mountainside following our recorded directions. We traversed several wooded knolls. After about five miles we dropped down to join a large, crystal clear stream flowing along through an open valley. The numerous pools were full of trout that we could see clearly under the water. We worked our way upstream through small waterfalls and shallow rock benches. The canyon began to narrow and we entered a section of the canyon where the cliff walls became higher and higher. We were completely alone. On that trip, and two subsequent trips into that canyon, we never met a single person. As we moved up the splashing, dancing stream we finally came to an ideal place to camp. There was a small, flat area nestled among the trees, just a few feet above the water. Directly across the shallow stream a spring bubbled out of the wall and ran through a little cluster of red flowers before joining the stream below. In this beautiful spot the red sandstone cliffs towered above us some fifteen hundred feet. Halfway up there was a ledge with several fully grown pines that, from our perspective, looked like miniature trees. Just above the campsite was a very unique formation called "the Subway". There the stream makes a thirty foot waterfall. The force of the water created a hole in the bedrock where the water drops down into a tunnel. For a distance of some one hundred feet the stream flows through this twenty foot high rocky tunnel. Here the water flows over flat bedrock. Through thousands of years bathtub sized holes have been carved out by trapped pebbles. There are four or five of these little Jacuzzi like tubs, full of swirling, sparkling water, just perfect for a rather chilly bath. We camped out in that magical place for four days. We did some exploring on up the beautiful canyon. It was as if we were Adam and Eve in a paradise miracle just for us.

The magic was still there when we returned again on two more trips. This was more than twenty years ago. Probably by now that special place is crawling with campers. We heard that the Great West Canyon is now a popular place for "canyoning", a sport where canyons are explored with ropes.

We were so very fortunate to have found that enchanted place when we did. It will always be a treasure in my box of memories.

SKIING: A SLIPPERY SLOPE

I was never what you would call a natural born athlete. I was most often sitting on the sideline, part of the "B" team in basketball and softball. However, there was one sport where I did hold my own; in track and field I did a little better. I was part of the running team and even broke the school record in long jump during my senior year in high school.

When I met Fred I was in my late thirties. He introduced me to a whole new variety of sports activities. Motorcycling, golfing and skiing. He was also just learning to ski, but in no time at all, was swooping down the slopes like a pro, and using perfect technique. I, on the other hand, felt insecure and clumsy. It took me about three years, and many ski trips, to finally master the art of parallel skiing. I felt more secure doing a "snow plow" position where your skis are diagonal to the slope with the front of the skis almost touching. A stance most people were able to discard within a few days.

Then there was my fiasco on the chair lift during my first ski trip. We were living in San Diego and the nearest well equipped ski resort was at Mammoth Mountain (part of the Sierra Mountain range). It was about a three hour drive. On this day the temperature was quite warm and summery. As we rode up the chairlift I unzipped my parka and stuffed my thick insulated mittens into the pocket of my parka. It was a lovely ride moving along some thirty feet above the people skiing below.

As we reached the top of the chairlift we approached a snow platform where we could slide out of the chair and touch our skis to the snow to ski away. As I tried to dismount my parka pocket with the mittens inside caught under the armrest on the chairlift. The next thing I knew I was hanging upside down, with my skies waving in midair. I had the horrifying vision of being slammed up against the tower where the empty chairs turned around to go back down the hill. Or, if surviving that, to find myself hanging from the chair upside down, suspended some thirty feet above the ground all the way to the bottom of the mountain. Fortunately, the alert lift operator saw my predicament and stopped the lift.

I was lifted up enough to disengage my caught parka. I landed in a heap on the snow below. Extremely embarrassed but thankful to still be all in one piece! So now you are wondering why I just didn't give up the whole idea of learning to ski. Well, it was not all that bad. First of all, I was in love with Fred and wanted to join him in his interests. Then, also as a lover of the outdoors, I found that spending time on a mountaintop with the whole world below and the sun sparking on the snow was pure delight.

And then there is the fun of sharing a condo with close friends, spending the evening together after a day of interesting adventure, sipping hot chocolate and sharing stories.

We continued skiing for some eighteen years. I did, finally, learn how to parallel ski and found it to be lots of fun. We tried many mountain ski resorts, even one year at Stowe, Vermont. However, our last trip was a disaster. We were skiing in Taos, New Mexico, with some friends. On the second day, as I came down a rather bumpy slope, I caught my uphill ski on a bump; I heard a terrible popping noise as I fell. It turned out to be my right knee, most of the ligaments and tendons had snapped. From the knee down my leg wobbled in all directions. The ski patrol with their sled, hauled me down the mountain. I didn't want to spoil the trip for everyone, so I stayed in our room with an ice pack. The following morning, during a ski lesson, Fred had another disaster. A novice skier plowed into him and tore the joint on his shoulder. He did continue skiing, but was in a lot of pain.

With the use of a wheelchair, we flew back to San Diego. The next day, I went into surgery to repair my torn up knee. I was in a total leg cast for three months. Fred also had surgery to reattach the tendon to his shoulder.

It did seem to be a sign that our days of skiing were over. It was a great adventure, which we recalled with fond memories. My torn up knee repair served me well for over twenty-five years. It was only last year that I had to have a total knee replacement surgery.

THE LUAU

The invitation was greeted with a great deal of enthusiasm. The entire staff, and families of the high school where I taught, was invited to an authentic Hawaiian luau to be held over the weekend. The location was at the vacation home of Angie and John Huffman, some fifty miles away in the back country of the San Diego area. Angie was a teacher in the English department and John had an important job in the school district's main office. They had been on a trip to Hawaii and wanted to show us how it was all supposed to be done. An entire pig, roasted underground in a bed of coals. Everything started the day before the fest, by giving the pork eighteen to twenty hours of cooking time. The result was an unbelievable production of tender, juicy meat. All the rest of us, some thirty to forty guests, were to bring a potluck dish either for the evening luau, or brunch the following day. People planned to sleep in their cars or in sleeping bags out under the stars.

On the day of the party the assortment of guests, with their pot luck dishes in hand, began to arrive at the cabin. John, and a couple of friends, had gone out the previous evening to get the pig roasting underway. We got busy setting up tables and chairs. Everyone was in a festive mood and looking forward to a great time.

Finally, the hour came for the great "unearthing" of the pig. Coals were carefully moved aside. The heavy aluminum foil was removed. There, for all to see, was a half cooked, intact pig of a rather unappetizing pale hue, still many hours short of being edible.

It seems that John, being a little wary of the prospect of raw meat being underground for so many hours, thought he would stay on the safe side. He made sure the pig was frozen solid before he buried it. He was subjected to ruthless teasing and ribbing. In fact, the teasing went on for several years. He was constantly being asked for his advice on numerous recipes.

However, the absence of a much anticipated meat dish did not spoil the party. The numerous potluck dishes were more than adequate. The highlight of the evening was when we gathered around a lovely big campfire to tell stories. The most interesting were related by Jo Alias, our Spanish teacher, who was raised in Mexico. She told us of many myths and legends common to the Mexican heritage. The following day we all headed back home. I don't know what happened to that poor abused pig. We never heard of him again. However, that was also the last, and only time, we attended an authentic luau where the main course was cooked underground. I will just have to take the word of those that say it is delicious.

ALL IN THE NAME OF RESEARCH

Now that marijuana has been legalized in Washington, I can tell this story. Besides that, even though this all happened in California in the early 1970s, I am sure the statute of limitations has expired after more than forty years!

I had become good friends with Peggy, another teacher in the same high school where I was teaching. Her husband, Tom, and my husband, Fred, also enjoyed being together. Even though we were twenty years older than Peggy and Tom, we got together on a regular basis.

One evening they invited us over for dinner. Tom had backed up a batch of brownies containing a generous amount of marijuana. Of course pot was illegal in California (and still is), but Tom explained to us that Fred, being a doctor, and I a teacher, it would be valuable for us to experience the effect of the drug. In this way we would be more alert to how it affected others. It was, after all, a scientific research assignment.

We went along with the plan and each had a couple of brownies. I understand that when one smokes pot it is more instantaneous, so one can control how much you take. Not so when added to food. It was not long before we began to feel the effects. Fred, usually quite reserved, became totally enthralled with the beauty and design of an ordinary teaspoon. He held the spoon up for us all to see and explained, in detail, every aspect of its beautiful design, which, of course, we found to be hilarious! In fact, we found almost everything to be hilarious! Another aspect of the drug was forgetting your train of thought. We would start a sentence and, halfway through, forget what we intended to say.

After about an hour we all felt very sleepy. The men stretched out on the furniture. Peggy got some big pillows and she and I slept on the carpeted floor. I remember noticing how loud the refrigerator motor sounded from the kitchen.

After an hour, or so, we all awoke. The buzz was gone and Fred and I drove home without any lasting effect. It was an interesting experience.

A few years later, Peggy was teaching a cooking class in home economics. The class of boys was preparing enchiladas, a Mexican dish where a filling is rolled up in a tortilla. The dish was ready to eat. As was her usual custom, she went from table to table to taste the food. As she approached one of the tables, she noticed the whole class became quiet. For any alert teacher this is a sign of mischief! The four boys were busy scarfing down the food. When she asked for a taste, they said it was so good they didn't want to share. She insisted, and upon cutting into the enchilada, she discovered a long green stem of marijuana inside. She commented that such a thing was not in the original recipe. She calmly stated that perhaps the school principal might like to have a taste of such an unusual recipe. The end result was that they boys were expelled for a few days, and no doubt learned a lesson.

This brings to mind another story about marijuana. When I was a child growing up in India, the Indian population liked to smoke the homemade cigarettes call "berri" cigarettes. They had no paper covering, but used tobacco leaves to shape the cigarette, much like a miniature cigar.

On one of my return trips to India I thought it would be fun to buy some berri cigarettes for my grown son Gary, who was a smoker, so I purchased two or three packs. I had no trouble going through customs. I explained to the official that they were Indian cigarettes. I am sure he thought this nice little old lady would not pull a fast one on him.

On Gary's next visit home he was out on our patio deck with a good friend. I thought this would be a good time to give him my surprise. When they lit up they started to laugh. Apparently those nice little berri cigarettes were, in reality, marijuana. They had a lot of fun teasing me about smuggling dope into the country with my little old innocent lady act.

I have never tried pot again, but it is fun to recall my various encounters with the stuff. In my way of thinking, a small glass of wine is sufficient and a lot more predictable.

TONY'S FAMOUS CHILI

We were living in San Diego when I married Fred. I had never met his family, so as a part of our honeymoon we flew back to Detroit, Michigan so I could be introduced to his clan. There were so many aunts and uncles, sisters and brother, mom and step-dad, that at first, I was quite overwhelmed. But soon I was welcomed in as a part of the family. Fred's stepdad, Tony, owned a bar and grill in Northwest Detroit which was famous for his homemade chili. Customers came from near and far to have a bowl. Of course, I was invited to taste his creation. It was very good, with an interesting complex flavor. When I asked Tony for the recipe he told me it was his secret, not to be shared.

Several years went by. Tony sold his business and retired to their home on the shores of Lake Huron. We were visiting them one summer when Tony asked if I still wanted that chili recipe. Now that he was retired he was willing to share it with me. First we went to the supermarket to buy the necessary ingredients. He felt the only way to buy was in huge quantities as he made the chili in large batches to store in the freezer to be used as needed. He bought ten pounds of ground beef, ten pounds of onions, four heads of garlic and so forth. I was amazed at the mass of ingredients we purchased. Later, in the kitchen, Tony proceeded to cook up his special dish. I sat by at the kitchen table to record his recipe. One of his secrets was that the chili was made with ten different spices. He had on hand large quart sized containers of spices he had brought home from the restaurant, now several years old.

As he chopped and fried, all the time telling me what he was doing. I was impressed by the large amounts of spices. One cup of black pepper, one cup of white pepper, one half cup of red pepper and so it went, through all ten of the spices. After several hours of simmering the chili was ready to be added to the cooked beans.

The result was just as good as I had remembered. I could hardly wait to try the recipe at home. Of course, I didn't want to make such a large amount, so very carefully reduced the amounts to cook enough for a meal or two.

My son Gary was home from college and he had invited a close friend to have dinner with us. It seemed to be a perfect time to try Tony's recipe. Even though I had reduced the amounts drastically, I had to purchase additional spices. I spent most of the day preparing the chili just as tony had shown me. As we sat down to eat, I bragged about how much they would love this very special creation. However, my enthusiasm didn't last long. As we all took our first bite, there was a great deal of choking, coughing and reaching for glasses of water. The concoction was totally uneatable. It was as if we were eating red pepper powder straight from the can. It didn't help that I was in for a lot of teasing about my marvelous creation. I was so chagrined, I dumped the whole lot into the garbage disposal; I then threw that darned recipe away.

But I did learn a lesson. Spices do lose their potency with age. Those old spices that tony used had, over the years, lost most of their flavor. I can only think that as that happened he increased the amount he used. So much for Tony's famous chili.

THE GRANITE DELLS

When Fred and I were married I had quite a project on hand. He had grown up a city boy with no experience with camping. On the other hand, I had grown up spending vacations in the "out of doors".

It didn't take long before he became an enthusiast for all the delights of camping. On one of our camping trips we discovered a location in the Mohave Desert in southern California. It is called the Granite Dells, an area of several square miles of undeveloped land. There, massive granite looms above a lush growth of desert shrubs and trees, with only a single dirt road winding through the huge slabs and peaks of gray rock. We set up camp in a lovely spot and enjoyed the quiet and solitude tor a couple of days. We climbed the rocks and never saw another human being.

One sunny warm morning I decided it would be a good day for a shampoo and bath. Of course, that meant heating up some water to use from a bowl and proceeded with a "sponge bath". Using the hood of our truck as a table and standing on a low flat rock I started to wash my hair. With no one else around I was at ease being stark naked. No sooner had I lathered up my hair than I heard the motor of a vehicle approaching rapidly. My eyes were full of soap, and before I could react, the intruders were there. In a cloud of dust they stopped right by me, I looked up through my stands of soapy hair to see two young men in an open Jeep. They were grinning from ear to ear as they surveyed me from top to bottom. Not a word was exchanged, after all what could be said? After a moment, but which seemed to me an endless time, they gave me a silent salute and drove away. I am sure they remember that day as one of their more interesting adventures. As for me, after all these years, the memory does bring a little chuckle too. Just another small incident from my store of memories.

SHARING OUR HABITAT

We had bought a two and a half acre lot in Alpine located in the foothills east of San Diego. We built a lovely home there with a view of undeveloped rolling hills and valleys. However, we were soon to discover we had moved into space already occupied by others. For ages past the wildlife had made it their home. We were the newcomers to the land. The construction contractors had not done a very good job of making our house critter proof. We soon found we were sharing our home with an assortment of creatures. The list included a couple of tarantulas, a lizard, one baby snake and, of course, numerous little field mice. The mice set up housekeeping in the attic. At night we could hear them racing up and down the ceiling over our bedroom. They also enjoyed the dry kibbles left out in the kitchen for our cat. We had dark brown tile on the floor and could see small trails of powdered kibbles leading away from the bowl. On occasion I would find little stashes of kibbles tucked down between the cushions of our living room furniture. After all, a clever plan to save for a future shortage.

Then there was the wildlife outdoors. The coyotes serenaded us nightly. In addition, we were visited by raccoons, skunks, foxes, snakes, bobcats and squirrels. The raccoons liked to fish in our goldfish pond. When they were occasionally successful we would find just a skeleton with head and tail still attached.

After a few years we noticed new visitors. Our bedroom was located at the end of the house. We began to hear rustling and high pitched squeaking noises during the night high up in the walls. The house exterior was made of board on board construction with spaces behind the outside boards. Apparently some bats had found an opening and set up a colony in those open spaces. We had pretty much solved the mice problem by sealing up the access holes where the mice were entering, but those bats were another problem altogether.

Upon enquiry, we were referred to the "bat lady" who was an advocate for bats. She told us of the benefit that bats provide, eating massive numbers of harmful insects. She said we shouldn't kill them, but she could tell us how to make them move away to a new location.

It seems that bats leave their roosts to hunt at night. When they return at dawn they find their roosting place by echo location, sort of like a radar beam. She told us that by hanging a large sheet directly in front of the opening to the roosting spaces the bats would not be able to locate the openings.

Using a tall stepladder we did as she suggested. At dawn the next morning we went outdoors to watch. Sure enough the returning bats were confused by the sheet and after flying around for a while, flew away again. We left the sheet in place for about a week to insure the departure of any immature bats that were still there. The plan worked well, our noisy visitors moved away to find a new home. Perhaps they found a location to live in peace. I do hope so.

We lived in our home in Alpine for twenty four years. A part of the joy of living there was sharing our space with the creatures that were already there before we came. For the most part, I think the benefit went both ways. We provided kibbles for the mice, goldfish for the raccoons and even a couple of our pet cats for the coyotes. A fair exchange for letting us share their world for a time.

TRAPPED

It was a family reunion. Fred and I had flown east to New Jersey to visit my brother, John, and his wife, Miriam. They were both college professors and free from their teaching duties for the summer. They had a vacation cabin located in the Adirondack Mountains in New York State. John was quite skilled in carpentry and had designed and built the cabin. It was quite a fine accomplishment, with a large sleeping loft, great room and even a screened porch. Three of his grown children and their families had all come from near and far to spend a weekend together and visit with their aunt Fran, who had come all the way from San Diego.

We had spent a wonderful day together, visiting and swimming in the fine pond, bulldozed out by John, located near the cabin and filled with bass, to the delight of the avid fishermen among the children. The evening had become a little too chilly to enjoy the campfire, so everyone moved indoors. The cabin was filled to the brim with some dozen people, laughing, telling stories and having a good time. Although the cabin had running water and electricity, it did not have a bathroom. So when I needed to answer the call of nature I slipped unnoticed from the room to go down the path to the outhouse situated some distance from the cabin. As I entered the small facility, much to my chagrin, the latch on the exterior of the door slipped into the locked position.

I had a problem; it was obvious no one would hear my shouts, as the cabin was at least fifty yards up the hill. I decided I would just have to wait until someone noticed I was not with the group. Now this was a pretty fancy toilet, as far as outhouses go. John, with his usual competence, had made a fine little building. It was painted green with the top of the walls open and screened all around. A bucket of lime was there to help keep down any unpleasant odors.

So I sat down on the bench to wait. Over an hour passed. I began to consider I might have to spend the night in my little prison. I wondered why no one else had found the need to use the outhouse. Of course, finally, as they were breaking up the party to go to bed, someone noticed I was missing. I heard my name called from the cabin porch. I yelled back and was soon rescued. There was much teasing and Jokes made about my predicament. John said he would replace the faulty latch.

Since that time, John did install an indoor toilet. It is some new fangled invention which turns the waste into biodegradable compost. So the possibility of a repeat of my predicament will not happen. But, even to this day, the whole family delights in recalling my evening spent locked in the outhouse.

LIVING WITH NATURE'S RULES

Saddlebrooke, a retirement community a few miles north of Tucson, attracted people from all over the United States. It is located in a beautiful valley with the 6,000-foot Catalina Mountains filling the view to the east. With two seasons of rainfall every year the surrounding Sonora Desert is abundant with desert loving shrubs and giant cactus.

At the time we moved into this community we were surprised to discover the abundance of wildlife in the area. It soon became evident for why this was so. Lush, green, grassy golf courses wound their way throughout the subdivision. All that good grass attracted rabbits and birds. This, in turn, attracted packs of coyotes, deer, snakes and even an occasional mountain lion! The human residents soon discovered that our own pets were considered part of the menu for hungry coyotes. Any cats that were foolish enough to stray outdoors were dispatched in short order. Small dogs were also fair game.

We moved there with our beloved miniature Schnauzer, Fritz. Even though we had a secure, fenced in back yard we didn't dare let Fritz out into the yard alone. We solved the problem by installing a doggy door, which led directly into a screened in ten foot by five foot box pushed up against the side of the house. In this way, night or day, our dog would be safe whenever he needed to answer the call of nature. Our neighbors did not all have a similar arrangement. Across the street a little Fox terrier was saved, just in the nick of time, by his distraught owner. A coyote jumped over a five foot wall, grabbed the unfortunate dog by the throat, and then attempted to carry the poor animal back over the wall. Our neighbors managed to drive the coyote away. The dog survived with a severely torn throat and a long laceration down his back. His wounds healed, except that subsequently the dog was unable to bark (not at all a bad thing as he had been a real "yipper"). We knew of several other residents who had their dogs taken from their fenced back yards.

On my daily, early morning walks with Fritz on the golf course, I had to remain alert for coyotes. Even though he was on a leash there was some danger he could be attacked, especially if there was more than one coyote. One morning I noticed two coyotes keeping pace with us about thirty feet off to the side. I pulled in the leash so as to keep Fritz walking close by my side. I thought it best to turn around and start for home. This did not deter the two coyotes, they continued to stalk us. Then they changed their strategy; they moved off across the fairway to some fifty feet away, but still moving parallel to us. I thought they had given up, so let out the leash to twelve or so feet. Suddenly, the two coyotes dashed across the distance between us heading straight for the dog! I ran over to him and snatched him up in my arms. Fortunately at this, the coyotes veered off. However, they did follow us the rest of the way home and hung around the back fence for a while to see if they might have another chance.

Our friends, John and Janet, lived a few blocks away. They had moved there from Michigan and were quite interested in all the southwestern type wildlife. One morning as John opened the front door, he discovered a large rattlesnake coiled up on the doormat. Leaving the door ajar, he dashed back to the kitchen to call Janet to come and see the snake! When they returned to the door there was no snake in sight. Now the question was, where had the snake gone? He felt really stupid for having left the door open. They searched cautiously throughout the house for any hiding snake but with no success. They felt a real sense of relief and decided it had moved away outdoors.

It wasn't until two days later, as John was walking through the living room to get his morning cup of coffee and saw the elusive rattlesnake coiled up right in the middle of the floor. It was more than a shock to imagine where it had been in the house for the last two days! Needless to say, pandemonium broke loose. The fire department was called and the snake was removed to do his hunting out in the desert.

This story might give you the impression that we all lived in terror of our wildlife neighbors. Nothing could be further from the truth! We loved the almost nightly songs of the coyotes calling to the moon. We loved seeing the gentle deer grazing on the golf course grass at dusk. We enjoyed watching the constant flow of rabbits, birds and other wild critters that shared our world. We had to learn how to make the rules for survival work because we were sharing our space with natures' wild creatures. And we humans would have to adapt and learn to live there in harmony.

THE CHANGES IN LIFE

It was during the summer of 2006 that I noticed Fred was not his usual energetic self. We took an extended trip in our motor home. Fred didn't want to move from campground to campground as we had done in the past. Other campers were aware of his limitations and offered to help out as we were breaking camp. On our return to Tucson, Fred was willing to sell the motor home.

Due to prolonged use of cortisone, that resulted in bone deterioration, he had to have both hips replaced. He also had a problem with blood clots and had to take a very expensive blood thinner.

We had decided we would move to Olympia, Washington in our later years to be close to my two sons, Gary and Dave. We had lived in Tucson for eleven years after our retirement from San Diego. It looked like the right time to move to Olympia while we were still able to pack up and drive.

We got a good price for our house (just before the 2008 recession). We moved into a retirement apartment building with meals and housekeeping included. It was a friendly place and it was great to be close to my sons and their families.

It turned out to be just the right time to make the move. Fred was still driving but never learned the way around the neighborhood. It was not long before he showed signs of memory loss. He was diagnosed with Alzheimer's disease in 2010.

Of course, being a physician, Fred knew what that meant! He never complained, but gradually just started to withdraw from life. It was so difficult to watch this vibrant, intelligent man who loved life and new challenges to just slip away into an impenetrable fog. He had no desire to exercise and first had to use a walker for balance and then soon a wheelchair. He became so weak and unsteady I was constantly concerned about him falling.

In the spring of 2013 I was scheduled for a knee replacement surgery. That last ski trip we took when I tore up my knee had finally caught up with me after 30 years. It meant that I would be incapacitated for several weeks and wouldn't b able to help Fred. We located an adult care private home. It was a loving and caring environment where he could receive excellent care.

After my knee surgery I was able to visit Fred on a regular schedule but the tragedy was that he felt I had abandoned him. In his confusion, he once asked me who my new boyfriend was. It is so very difficult to make the one you love so much understand what is best for him.

Fred passed away in June of 2014. He had just lost the will to live and stopped eating. I miss him so very much. My joy is remembering all those wonderful times we had together. He opened so many new horizons for me for which I will be forever grateful. Perhaps he is waiting for me just beyond the bend.

ALASKA ADVENTURE

In July I took an eight day cruise along the Inland Passage to Alaska. I was with my son, daughter-in-law and a good friend from Tucson. We sailed on a celebrity line cruise ship that carried 2,800 passengers and a crew of 800. I was impressed by the efficiency of the crowd control, with several dining rooms and an extensive cafeteria open 18 hours a day, you could get good food any time you wanted. The evening entertainment was a delight. Dancers, singers with a band, acrobats, comedians, magic shows, along with an enthusiastic, naturalist made the evenings full of fun.

We signed up for several excursions on shore including a hike to the fast shrinking Mendenhall glacier, a train ride from Skagway to follow the monumental trek of the thousands of men seeking the gold of the Klondike. From the previous experience of prospectors starving to death, the Canadian government required that each person have one ton (2 thousand pounds) of food before going into the gold fields. This meant that the gold seekers had to make 30 to 40 treks up the trail, which was some forty miles of steep assent. Some men bought horses to carry the load, but of the 3 thousand horses all but a few died on the trail. In the end it turned out that only a few lucky ones found gold, most were left with disappointment for all their efforts. Our last evening was a visit to the Butchart Gardens in Victoria, BC.

But for all of us, the highlight of the trip was in Ketchikan to see the bears catching salmon from a stream on a clear sunny day. Our journey began by boarding a small eight passenger seaplane with a lovely young woman as our pilot. We took off from the water in the bay and flew up the coast a few miles. Below us the ocean was full of large and small wooded islands that were all part of a national park. We soon landed in a small bay of an island and taxied up to dock. We were met by a naturalist guide and walked up a narrow path to a platform overlooking a large stream full of rapids. The naturalist told us that the bears we would see were not the Kodiak grizzlies that stand up to 10 feet tall, but the smaller black bear weighing 4 to 5 hundred pounds. (We were all a little relieved to get that information.) Within a few minutes we say a mother bear with 2 small cubs appear at a spot just below our platform, not more that 30 yards from us. She sent the cubs up a tree for safekeeping and set about the task of catching a salmon. The salmon were crowded together in pools just below the rapids. They seemed to be aware of the bear, for occasionally one would attempt to leap up over the rapids. Not as the nature pictures on TV shows of bears catching salmon after salmon. It took about 15 minutes for the bear to make a successful catch. When she caught a fish she took it back to share with the cubs. Two different times another larger bear came too close to where she was with her cubs; she made short work of showing them they were not welcome! They ambled off upstream to find their own fishing spot. One of the cubs, being a little more adventurous, kept coming down the tree to see what mom was doing. She would have to stop her fishing to send him back up the tree.

The bears were certainly aware of our presence, but seemed to be unperturbed and intent on catching fish. The naturalist told us that if you ever meet a bear face to face it was not a good idea to play dead as we have been told to do, the bear would just see you as an easy meal. Also, you should not run, as bears can run a lot faster than you can. Climbing trees is not an option as bears are better at that too. The best thing to do is to back away slowly and try not to show fear. On our way back up the trail we saw no bears close by. The naturalist had some pepper bear spray, just in case. On the way back to the dock he showed us a clearing close to the road where he had pitched a tent. He lives there all through the summer months. (I guess he must have signed some sort of peace treaty with the bears)

The time I spent on the cruise was a wonderful time to enjoy the beauty of nature and spend precious time with family and friends. I was so glad to have had the opportunity to take that trip.

— MUSINGS —

WE'RE NOT "THERE" YET

Today the news is full of the intolerance, hatred and violence of humans against one another. The use of roadside bombs, suicide IED's (individual explosive devices) and lone gunmen targeting innocent bystanders, gives one a feeling of despair. In warfare we send our finest into battle to be maimed and slaughtered for the purposes of greed and arrogance. It seems we are determined to develop even more deadly means for killing one another. History tells us this has been so down through the short span of time since the appearance of homo-sapience. It is only that as we invent ever more lethal weaponry, we are able to kill each other with greater efficiency.

On the other hand, mankind is also capable of so much that is good. With the complexity of brain development we have moved far beyond the knowledge necessary for basic survival. We have the capacity for creating art, music, literature and other forms of creativity that lift us all to joy and inspiration. But even more than that, mankind has found the capacity for compassion, empathy and selfless service for the care and needs of others. The lives of countless individuals, who have dedicated their lives to make life better for others, is truly the pinnacle of nobility.

So it seems the development of our superior intelligence can enable us to succeed towards destruction or nobility. For all my distress at the cruelty of man, I do see some signs that we are moving in the right direction. Even within my brief lifetime I have seen the development of intolerance for the massacre of innocent civilians in warfare. During World War II bombs were dropped on cities killing thousands of non-combatants. This "collateral" destruction was considered just the cost of fighting a war. Now any collateral deaths are deemed intolerable. It is, at least, the first step on the road to harmony.

Of course I am not the first to dream of a world where we all could live with love, compassion and tolerance for others beliefs and desires. Perhaps, if the best of our potential prevails, we will slowly evolve into a world where wars and killing will be obsolete. We would use our creative powers to invent things that would improve the lives of all who live on this very special planet. But we are not there yet!

LIFE'S REGRETS

As someone in her middle eighties, I have a lot of life to remember; The very special privilege of a childhood in India with all the interesting adventures that provided; The joy and stimulation of finding loving and compatible life partners in marriage; The rewarding challenge of raising two boys; The satisfaction of being involved in a teaching career which brought with it a world of fulfillment with hardly a dull moment; But, perhaps most of all, a lifetime of close friends and family to give it all a very special richness and joy.

But, as I look back over my life I do have a few regrets the first one is, as a child, I wasn't given the awareness of the very special history and unique richness of Indian culture. Perhaps it was a part of the "British Raj" mentality that placed us in the position of superiors among the Indian population. It was as if the country's rich culture was due to ignorance. It wasn't until I became an adult that I learned, and became aware, of the richness and diversity of India. Of course as children we just thought our lives were nothing out of the ordinary.

My second regret is that I never pursued my love of acting on the stage. I have always been a bit of a "ham". Then as a senior in high school I found a marvelous outlet for all that in drama class. As the lead in Jane Eyre I discovered the fun of pretend. Throughout my adult life I kept returning to the idea of getting involved in neighborhood theater groups. I never imagined I would have liked the life of a professional actress but I do regret not giving local theater a try.

Another regret has to do with animals. For my whole life I have loved animals of many species. Our list of pets has ranged from fish through reptiles (such as lizards, turtles and snakes) to rats, chipmunks, ducks and even hawks. This was all in addition to the more conventional cats and dogs. It is my belief that developing close relationships to animals is a valuable and rewarding way to understand our close connection with all other living creatures. However, I do have to admit that some of those pets we had didn't connect very well! Even though we had such a wide variety of animals, we never had a horse. Without a doubt, not only are horses one of the most beautiful of all creatures, but they are capable of being able to develop a special close relationship to us. I do regret I never had a chance to experience such a relationship. The few horses that I have ridden only made me feel a little intimidated; I never got the knack of communication. How wonderful it would be to have a big old horse as a friend!

I am sure there are many other regrets that, at this age, I just don't remember. Besides, who likes to fret over the past? It is so much better to recall all those good times. If I happened to believe in reincarnation I would make sure to include these experiences my next time around!

GROWING PAINS

Adolescence is one time in your life when some of your body parts grow faster than others, resulting in a lot of awkwardness. In a family photograph taken when I was twelve and my brother, Stan, two years older, shows him standing with a sappy grin on his face, his pants ending several inches above his ankles and his jacket sleeves well above his wrists. And me, sitting on a stool, with skinny legs crossed and oversized feet sticking out into space.

In fact, for Stan, it seemed almost impossible to keep up with his rapid growth. Every three to four months mother had to buy longer pants. As for me, besides having long gangly arms and legs, it was my feet that kept growing.

We were on furlough for eighteen months in America. My parents were missionaries in India. In India it was difficult to buy readymade clothes and shoes. My mother, being a very wise and practical lady, came on a solution. Since my feet seemed to grow into a longer size every six months, she bought up a supply of graduating sizes for me to grow into. That way, on our return to India, the shoe problem would be taken care of. Now these shoes were very practical sturdy Buster Brown types. Not anything like the wishes of a clothes conscious teen-ager.

As it turned out, on our return to India, my feet stopped growing. So what to do with three pairs of too large shoes. For mother said, "not to worry". She just stuffed tissue paper in the toes so I could still wear them. The only problem was that without feet reaching the ends, the toes began to curl up. How I hated those ugly shoes. I did everything possible to wear them out. In one instance, "accidentally" losing them in a mountain stream. Finally, the day came when those cursed shoes were gone and I could wear more stylish footwear.

And then there is the story about my hair. I was blessed with having an abundance of thick golden brown hair. However, it did take a lot of care, as it was straight and the fashion of the period was to have curly hair. So at the age of thirteen, mother talked me into having it cut and permed. That was when beauty shops had electric permanent wave machines. They had no control over how much heat was applied. The result was a disaster! In place of my soft long hair, I had a short halo of frizzed- up, over-permed hair. Thank goodness it did finally grow out. I never had another permanent until I was an adult and able to get a soft, gentle perm.

It is fun to remember those aches of our growing pains and know they are all in the past. They seemed to be so important at the time. Just a look back at child's perspective.

CUSSING

When you get to be my age, you have a lot of time to sit around and think. Sometimes that is good, it gives one the chance to remember her sweet times in the past. It also provides a chance to figure out some of the enigmas of life. But perhaps after reading this, you may decide it would be better if the author could find something worthwhile to do, so as to not think so much!

For what I have been thinking about is what is the reason and purpose of cussing. It is generally agreed that young pre-teen age boys (and sometimes, girls) start to use profanity as a means to assert their independence. It tells really "macho" to string a lot of cuss words together to tell your friends how tough you are. Of course, the smart kids will not try this in front of their parents.

Then there are those individuals that, as they grow older, seem to carry on the "art" of cussing to the extreme. Around their peers it appears really cool to use the "F" word at least two or three times in every sentence. I have a suspicion that this is just a sign of laziness. That way they don't need to develop a large vocabulary.

But it seems to me there is another side to this whole question of cussing. It does actually serve a purpose. I see it as sort of a safety valve to vent anger or frustration. When you smash your thumb with a misdirected hammer blow, or someone cuts you off when you're driving, a muttered little tried and true cuss word is preferable to kicking in a wail or putting your fist through a window. No real harm is done and it makes you feel much relieved.

So it is here that I am going to tell you about my own favorite cuss words. I am not sure why they reached that status. I do remember the first time I cussed in front of my very proper parents. We were all about to leave the house for church. That was when our cat decided she would jump out the upper story bedroom window to explore the adjacent porch roof. It was obvious that I would have to climb out the window to retrieve her Sunday dress and all! I blurted out "Damned cat"! The words hung in the air, not to be reswallowed. However, a bit to my surprise, I got no reprimand. Perhaps my parents were thinking the same darned thing!

So, to get back to my cussing. I do have three very tried and true words to let off steam when the need arises. They are S---, P---, F---! It depends a little on who else is around on whether I say them out loud. I try to give the impression of being a lady, so there are seldom times when such words would be appropriate. I have tried, on occasion, just saying the initials "SPF", but that just doesn't work as well as a venting device. I have even thought of cleaning up the whole phrase. How about "bowel movement, urination, and sexual intercourse"? But you can see somehow that really loses something along the way. It just doesn't have the right "punch".

So now you know about my "dark side". Besides that, you have probably concluded this old gal needs something to do to keep her busy. Who knows what other weird thoughts she will come up with next?

MUSINGS ON MOTHERING

In our Biology classes we were told all about the natural instincts that are common to all living creatures. One of the most powerful of these instincts is that of mothering and nurturing: All in the attempt to perpetuate the continuation of the species. We all seem to delight in the sight of the mother, regardless of species, caring for and training her offspring. Also we all seem to be emotionally responsive to babies of any kind. It is interesting that this instinct to nurture can even cross species. Such as a dog nursing and caring for kittens, etc. Even to the extreme situation of a female wolf suckling and nurturing human babies.

When it comes to humans, our nurturing is the most prolonged of all. Even among the more intelligent and complex demands of living, the longer the training period. Primates and elephants, for example, are not adults until the age of four or five years. Of course, for humans, not only do we have a very complex and extensive culture to teach our young, but in addition, communication by advanced language.

This brings me to one of the more interesting aspects of human mothering. It seems that mothers have an instinctive way of talking to babies. I am not referring to "baby talk" where adults thinking the small child will understand better if words are pronounced as babies learn to speak. But the use of a high pitched gentle, sweet voice reserved for babies only. Perhaps you have never been aware of this; it is only used by women, not by men. This special voice even has its own name. It is called "motherese". This has been the subject of some scientific research and It has been determined that motherese is a worldwide phenomenon. Mothers and women use this high-pitched voice in every culture and language group!

Since hearing of this, I have made a point of noticing how women speak to babies. It really is fun to observe. I hate to admit it, but I am guilty of even talking to my cat (as well as former pets) in motherese.

I suppose it all just goes to show us that we really are tied rather closely to those basic instincts that have made us the most successful species on our planet, at least for the comparatively short time we have been around.

MY LEGACY

As I approach the last years of my life, I have the need to consider what, after all, has my life been all about? Has my life had a purpose? When we are young our thoughts and concerns are filled with the challenges of daily life and how we can best reach our goals and dreams. For me, as I reflect back on my life, many of those dreams have come to fruition. I was so very fortunate to have been born into a family full of love and mutual support. But whatever fate has given us, it all comes down to what purpose do we have for the brief span of time we have on this earth. How, after all, should we spend these days we have to live?

When I was a young adult I had a chance to have one of those meaningful conversations with my dad—a very wise and gentle man. I asked him how one could know if one had lived a successful life? His answer was very simple. He said his measure of a successful life was that when it was over, was the world a better place because of that life. I have kept and pondered that thought in my heart throughout the years. There are a very few special individuals who, because of outstanding wisdom or talent, have made our world a vastly better place. The founders of our great religions, artists, inventors, writers, musicians and so many others who have touched our lives for the good of all mankind.

But for the rest of us, just the ordinary kind of person with no great talents or skills, what can we do to leave a positive legacy? I think it all comes down to love and our human capacity to care for one another, to give of our time and efforts to bring joy and comfort to others. This can be the purpose for our lives. Just imagine how different the world would be if everyone on our planet tried to live that way! Of course, this is no new idea. This has been the message and plea of countless wise leaders down through the ages, but it still remains such a powerful concept. This love has to also include understanding and a tolerance to let others have their own beliefs and ways of life.

So what do I hope to leave as my legacy? Only the simple memory that I have left some joy and love in the hearts of those whose lives I have touched. I have tried, in my small way, to make this world a little better for me having been here. Our time here together is only a flash in the total span of time--perhaps, in the end, of little consequence. Nevertheless, I choose to believe each life does have a purpose. To make mankind more loving and caring is within the capacity of us all. For, in the end, what could be a more noble purpose and legacy to leave for those who are yet to come?

THE GENERATION GAP

I can remember when I was a teenager, my mother's comments about the music being played by the "Big Bands" of the 1940's. She felt that they just didn't write any good music anymore, certainly not like what was played when she was young. I was listening recently to a program on television. There was a group of talented guitarists playing music they had composed. Although they were marvelous musicians, what they played was awful! The same loud theme played over and over again. I could only bear to listen for a few minutes before turning to another channel. I thought of my mother's comments and had to smile. I too, decided they just don't know how to write good music anymore.

But that is only a part of the present day generation gap. With the phenomenal growth of technology, the gap has become a vast canyon! Facebook, I-Pads, texting, instant messaging, twittering, etc. A virtual explosion of communication. A possible 24 hour a day contact with hundreds of cyber space friends. I willingly concede the benefits of available information and keeping in touch with loved ones.

But from the sidelines, I see some negative aspects. What about time to spend alone, to revitalize one's spirits without demands of constant contact. Also time spent in real, meaningful conversation face to face with family and friends. Not everything abbreviated to texting.

So, you can plainly see, I am a chasm away from plugging into this younger generation. But don't feel sorry for me. I actually relish my old fashioned ways. I am content to watch the world fly by; just leave me a good book, an interesting and stimulating program on TV, and close, dear friends and family to be with. The younger generation can conquer new worlds without my help. I did my share—now it's up to them.

LEARNING TO COOK

During my childhood the whole process of meal preparation was not a part of my training. Growing up in India with a hired man to cook for us and most of my time spent in boarding school meant I had minimum exposure to the art of cooking. I do recall that mother did enjoy baking cakes. This was her specialty; she was famous for her light, delicious cakes. But that was the only thing she prepared for special occasions.

My first attempt at cooking was while mother and I were visiting with a friend of hers. I was about eleven years old, the same age as Susan, and a daughter of mother's friend. While our mothers were visiting, we decided it would be fun to bake a cake for them. We didn't feel a recipe was necessary as we had often seen how it was done. We confidently mixed up flour, sugar, butter, eggs and cocoa with enough milk to make a batter. Two things we forgot were baking powder for leavening and oiling the cake pan. Much to our chagrin and disappointment, the result of our efforts was a terribly heavy, solid hard plaster like mass that stuck to the pan like glue. That did teach me that perhaps recipes did have a purpose after all!

There was one dish I did prepare with some success. As a teenager there were no potato chips to be bought in our town in India. This was a great disappointment for me as they were (and still are) one of my favorite snacks. My attempts at potato chip making were very time consuming and only moderately successful. To cut potatoes with a knife into thin slices was not easy. The slices had to be soaked in cold water to crisp then blotted dry before frying in hot oil. It was a true labor of desperation.

As we had no readymade clothes available, it was necessary to have our clothes made by a tailor. I soon learned to make my own dresses and by the time I entered high school I was making all of my clothes. So it seemed natural that I would decide on a home economics major when I started college. However, the foods and food preparation part of home econ had little appeal for me. It seemed that all the effort of preparing a fancy meal, so quickly consumed, had no lasting benefit to enjoy.

When I got married, at the age of 20, I was in for some challenging kitchen experiences. I remember the first expensive steak I tried to cook was so over-cooked it resembled a dry slab of wood, almost inedible. Then there was the day I tried to cook a live lobster. I got the large pot of water to the boiling temperature, and then I timidly held the wiggling lobster by its antennae to lower it into the pot. The minute the poor thing felt the boiling water on its tail it jumped right back out splashing scalding water everywhere. When I finally retrieved it from the floor, I learned that it works a lot better to immerse the lobster headfirst.

Another learning experience came from my ignorance about how to store leftovers. I had prepared a nice meal of roast beef. We had a very small refrigerator so I figured since the meat was cooked it wouldn't need to be refrigerated. I placed the large leftover roast on the counter and covered it with a dishtowel. A couple of days later, thinking I would make some nice French dip sandwiches for dinner, I picked up the towel. To my total surprise and horror, I discovered the whole roast was a mass of wiggling maggots! A lesson never to be forgotten.

Through all the years, since those first days of learning to cook, I have had some failures and many successes in the art of food preparation. I have discovered the pleasure and satisfaction people find from eating a well prepared meal makes it worth the effort. My initial uncertainty in cooking has, through the years, become an interesting and fulfilling experience. I find real pleasure in producing dishes that others find good to eat.

FOUR SCORE YEARS AND STILL COUNTING

It seems quite remarkable, and even a little shocking, to realize I have reached the age of biblical lore: The age of all those bible stories of wise, ancient men who imparted their wisdom and counsel.

Where have all those years gone? It seems that only a few short years ago I was is the middle of working and raising children. As for the twenty-five years since I've retired from teaching, I could swear it hasn't been more than ten. Why is it that the older one gets the faster the years fly by? But, hey, I'm not complaining, under all these wrinkles and broken down body parts, is a still young spirit looking for some fun and new adventures.

As I think back over my lifetime, I realize what a special era the last half of the twentieth century has been. We have been called "the greatest generation", but perhaps that was due to the circumstances we found ourselves in. We were raised by parents who had lived through the liberated twenties, only to be challenged by the hardships of the great depression. They gave us the training to be careful and spend wisely. Our next lesson came with World War II. The whole nation was caught up in the war effort with sacrifice and dedication to maintain our cherished way of life. The years following the end of the war were full of opportunity. The economy was booming, jobs were easy to find and housing was plentiful and affordable. America led the world in technology and innovations. For the first time, every household could have modern appliances. With the establishment of airlines, anyone could travel quickly and easily to anywhere on earth. Our children could play outdoors without fear of abductions, to organize and develop games of competition or imagination. We even took steps to move towards a more just and equal society of civil rights oh.

I know what you are thinking. It was not all a bed or roses and, of course, you are right. But one of the good things about memory is that one is inclined to remember only the good stuff!

I do have my concerns about the future. Our time of opportunity has been replaced with frustration and conflict. The current generation of youth can't find jobs. The global-wide market has brought on furious competition in education, manufacturing and research. With the fantastic advances in communication and global development, the world will soon lose its diversity and become a homogeneous blend of food, clothing and customs. The climate change to come will present another whole set of challenges.

The list could go on and on. I guess perhaps I don't mind being one of the four-score and plus year olds. I really wouldn't want to, or have the energy for, working on these problems of the future. I am content to turn the reins over to the young. My wish is for those who follow, a world full of opportunity, potential and diversity as the one I had the privilege of sharing with my generation.

THOSE DARNED PACIFIERS

Having given birth to my two sons in the late forties and early fifties, my authority on babies was Dr. Spock. We were convinced that if we followed his advice we would be able to breeze through motherhood with nary a bit of trouble.

One of his mandatory admonitions was the use of a pacifier. This was because babies have a built in need for sucking. Not only as a way to get nourishment, but also for comfort and serenity. As a conscientious mom, a pacifier was pushed into my babies' mouths within minutes after birth.

It did seem to work well. The little tykes would be content, happily sucking on those rubber nipples for hours. I soon discovered it was essential that the pacifier was in place in order for the baby to fall asleep. This did create a bit of a problem. If at any time during the night the pacifier was dislodged, there would be loud desperate wailing until it could be retrieved and back in place once more.

I remember one night at a drive-in movie Gary, our firstborn, was all snuggled down sleeping in the back seat of our car. Halfway through the movie he lost his pacifier. Midst loud wailing, with dirty looks from nearby moviegoers, we scrambled around searching for that miserable little thing, so as to settle the unhappy baby down again.

But that was only the start of difficulties. As Gary grew older, into his first and even second year, his need for his "wa-wa" was undiminished. Pacifiers of that era were not all molded together in one piece, as they are today. The nipple and ring base were separate parts; Gary got very adept at pulling them apart. With the potential of swallowing the pieces, it was necessary to constantly replace (almost daily) the much loved, and absolutely essential for sleep, device. As time went by, I envisioned Gary checking into kindergarten with a stupid pacifier stuck in his mouth. That didn't happen, for eventually, by the age of three, he was finally willing to give it up.

So, three and a half years later, along came our second child, Dave. We went through the same procedure with baby Dave also addicted to his wa-wa . However, I had learned a thing or two along the way. For when, at the age of about one year, Dave began to tear the pacifier apart, I had a brilliant idea. I took the little culprit over to the trash bin. I explained that as his wa-wa was broken and it would have to be thrown away. We both stood over the trash feeling very sad. I took him back several times to look at the poor broken wa-wa. Later when nap time came he started to cry for his wa-wa. But with my sad little reminder of its fate, he finally settled down to sleep. Within a day or two, the wa-wa was forgotten, much to my relief.

Perhaps our dear Dr. Spock should have outlined this method of breaking the pacifier addiction. I do wonder a little how moms of today, with these new one-piece indestructible wa-was, are coping. I haven't noticed any school kids walking around with pacifiers stuck in their mouths. Perhaps they are hidden away in their backpacks to be available when life becomes too stressful.

THOUGHTS ON FRIENDSHIP

It seems to be a part of our DNA, this need we have for friends. A newborn baby is totally self-centered as a way to survive. But even at that early stage of life the security of a mother's arms provides joy and comfort. Our first friends are our family, but soon we find pleasure in other children. This stage is such a vital step to self confidence. Children can be so cruel. If a child is different in any way, the teasing and ridicule can destroy a child's self esteem and lead to a life of insecurity and self doubt. This is where parents can play such an important role by emphasizing the good qualities that every child possesses.

But the art of being a good friend is not simple. The first rule is learning not to be self-centered. I have observed through the years that very beautiful women and handsome men are able to attract a group of admirers without putting out much effort. This is a shame, for it takes some effort to develop the skills for nurturing friendships. When their beauty fades they find they have no friends, for they have never learned how to be a friend.

Other traits of being a friend are empathy, sensitivity and being a good listener. And then, of course, we are drawn to people who have the same interests as our own. This all leads to finding pleasure in their company.

My mother was a very friendly and outgoing person. She was genuinely interested in almost everyone she met. She could develop an intimate conversation with a person she might meet on a short crosstown bus ride. However, as the wife of a minister, she once told me that she couldn't become a close friend of anyone in the church congregation. It was important that she treat every member as equal. She made up for it with a vast network of correspondence. She kept in touch with two hundred, or more, friends on a regular four to five times a year letter exchange. The mailman once told her she got more personal mail than all other customers combined on his route. I often think of how she would have loved the whole idea of texting where you can keep in instant touch! She lived to be ninety-four. One of the sorrows of her later life was that she outlived so many of her friends. Her well used address book was filled with crossed out names of ones who had passed away.

I have not been that good in keeping in touch with friends through the years. As I have moved to new locations, the friends who were an important part of my life have a way of fading into the past, only to be remembered at Christmas time. However, for a few of my closest friends, the bond we had has endured; our close connection and love has continued throughout time. For me, this handful of friends goes as far back as my childhood days in school. We still are fortunate to be able to get together. It is as if all the years apart are not significant. We find that bond again and it is as if we had never been apart.

This little article on friendship would not be complete without the mention of what pets have contributed to my life. I do feel- sorry for those who have not had the joy of having an animal friend. My list of pets throughout my life includes a wide and strange variety; from lizards and snakes, turtles and mice, parakeets and hawks to the usual cats and dogs. Some of these critters can't give you much love, but they all teach one to care for another's needs. Of course of all these pets, cats and dogs are there to be our companions. The many cats and dogs I have cared for have created such a close bond that when they go it is heartbreaking. Especially now that I am alone. My little dog, Pebbles, brings me much joy and comfort as a companion. His presence gives me someone to share my days and nights. He is a real special blessing.

After all these years I find my perspective has changed. Where once I was concerned with accumulation of material things, I now realize the only things that really matter in life are close family ties and dear friends. Of course, it is fortunate that I have the means to live a life of comfort. But in the long run it is our loving relationships with others that bring us the most joy and comfort.

A CHANGE IN PERSPECTIVE

It is interesting that a child often is unaware of what adults feel is important. As a child growing up in India, I saw the poverty, overcrowding and lack of sanitation as quite normal. That was just the way other people lived, no big deal.

In our home, and boarding school, things were different. All was kept clean and sanitary. Our water, and even milk, was boiled before drinking. We were taught never to eat food in the bazaar unless we saw it being cooked. The thinking was that the native population had built up an immunity to the pathogens commonly found, and so could come in contact with them without becoming ill. That does seem to be true. When one travels to a less developed country, it is wise to not drink the water, or eat fresh produce, without first disinfecting it.

After having moved to America when I was seventeen my first return visit back to India was a real shock! It had been twenty-five years since I had left and the population had almost doubled. Of course, so much was still the same. The exotic smells of spices, the jostling crowds, the rickshaws and sacred cows roaming the bazaars. But I had not remembered the filth and lack of hygiene.

One morning we were wandering through a crowded bazaar. One of the venders had set up a lemonade stand. In addition to having a large container full of lemonade there was a row of glasses lined up on a shelf. We stopped to watch as he served his customers. As they finished the drink they returned the glass to the proprietor whereupon he squatted down to wash the used glass in the drainage gutter at his feet. He then carefully rinsed the glass in a small bowl of cleaner water on the counter. It was then dried with a well used dirty towel and placed on the shelf to be used by the next customer. Needless to say, none of our group opted to buy the lemonade!

A few days later our tour group was to take a train to visit the famous Taj-Mahal. As we waited on the platform I saw a pakora vendor approaching.

Pakoras are one of my favorite Indian savories. It is made of shredded raw potatoes mixed in a spicy batter and dropped by spoonfuls into hot oil and fried until crisp. I was delighted to have a chance to taste, once again, the "real thing".

The vendor was fully equipped with a small charcoal stove to keep the cooking oil hot. I watched, with great anticipation, as he started to fry the pakoras. He then reached down on a low shelf of his cart to get the filthiest rag I have ever seen. He proceeded, with a great flourish, to use the rag to wipe out a bowl where the cooked savories were to go. Suddenly those tasty pakoras lost their appeal. As graciously as possible, I declined the much loved pakoras; I didn't ask for the money to be returned. I am sure the vendor chalked it up to another one of those strange ways of tourists.

Probably, as a child, I wouldn't have hesitated a minute, after all I had seen the savories being cooked. It just goes to show how one's perspective does change!

THOSE CLEVER KANGAROOS

The other day I was watching one of those nature programs on TV. It was about how marsupials have all developed a pouch on their tummies. That has eliminated a whole bunch of problems. For instance: giving birth is no big thing. When the fetus has developed enough, the little fellow just crawls out and finds his way up into mom's pouch. There he can latch onto a constant milk supply and keep safe and warm. No fuss, no bother. Mom can just go about her life, eating, running around and doing whatever she wants without a worry in the world about caring for her helpless infant. Then, when the baby grows older, he can hop in and out of the pouch whenever there is danger or to just get a snack or take a little nap. Mama kangaroo can transport him around without a bit of trouble.

So all this got me to thinking how cool it would be if we humans had pouches too. To begin with, childbirth would be a snap. No hospital needed. When the fetus was ready he could just pop out and we could settle him right into the pouch. We humans seem to really admire the containers that are the source of our babies milk supply. It probably wouldn't be very pleasing if woman's breasts hung down long enough to tuck into our tummy pouches. But other than that, just think how convenient it would be to have a warm, handy place to carry the baby. No need for strollers or car seats, the little guy would be safe and secure.

I do see a few necessary modifications to our clothing. Mothers would have to wear skirts and pants made of stretch fabrics with elastic waistbands. Also, having a pouch would not do much to enhance the figure, but perhaps having a lovely big potbelly would become a sign of beauty. It also seems to me that having a pouch could have other real benefits. Even for women without babies it could serve as a purse. No more leaving valuables behind in stores and restaurants. It would even be handy for carrying things we buy; no more hassles with shopping bags.

But I can see a potential problem. After years of use and stretching our pouches would probably begin to sag. We would have to invent some sort of Velcro fastening to hold it all in shape.

But of course I know this is all just silly speculation. We are as we are, and I am the first one to say we are designed very well. But it is kind of fun to imagine how life would be if we had pouches like those lucky kangaroos.

THE WRINKLES ROADMAP

I watch the commercials on TV for beauty products. The beautiful models have flawless, porcelain like skin. Not a blemish or hint of a wrinkle. I suspect this is not really how they look. Probably the use of wrinkle fillers and foundation creams have much to do with their exquisite appearance, but we are led to believe this is the standard attainable for all who wish to be beautiful. In addition, our culture seems to be obsessed with Botox injections, face lifts, and facial exfoliation, all with the goal of preventing or at least postponing, the appearance of a single wrinkle.

Perhaps because, at my age, I have a face full of wrinkles, I want to express an alternate point of view about wrinkles. It seems to me that faces with wrinkles are quite interesting. As we go through life we leave a map of our experiences on our faces. The joys, the sorrows, the days outdoors in the sun and wind, each leave their mark. Some faces reveal a lifetime of stress and worry. Some, more fortunate, show traces of a life full of joy and laughter.

I think it just takes a new perspective to appreciate the beauty of a face with a story to tell. So stop bemoaning those wrinkles you see in the mirror. Just be glad you're still around and be proud of your "Road Map face!"

Besides that, be comforted with the fact that all those flawless, wrinkle free faces, will look just like ours, if they live long enough to reach old age. The passage of time will negate any efforts to keep the wrinkle free face.

THE OLD OAK TREE SPEAKS

It all happened so long ago, when I was real young, that I don't remember it very well. But it seems to me I was planted in a big back yard by a young man and woman; they called each other Steve and Ann. They lived in a brand new house at the other end of the yard.

At first Steve put water on me almost every day, but pretty soon my roots grew long enough that I could find plenty of water deep underground. That made me grown big and strong. It was fun when the neighborhood birds started to build their nests on my branches. So much noisy bustling about feeding their babies and teaching them how to fly.

And then there were the squirrels who loved to gather my acorns. It was fun to watch them burying the acorns in secret little stashes on the ground. One family of squirrels even had their babies in a deep little hole they dug out under my roots.

It wasn't long before Steve and Ann started having babies too. On warm sunny days they liked to sit under my branches. I was so proud to make a place where they could enjoy the cool shade. Steve hung some ropes from one of my outstretched branches to make a swing for the growing children to play on.

But my favorite thing was when the children grew big enough to climb up into my branches. They played all sorts of games like Tarzan castaways, pirates, and mountain climbing. I had one branch that hung pretty close to the ground.

The children liked to climb way out on the end where the leaves are and bounce up and down like a bouncing ball. I loved to hold them in my arms.

Then it seemed in no time at all, those children grew up and didn't seem to want to play in my arms anymore. They all still liked to sit in my shade on a warm day, but I missed their climbing games. Then one early evening one of the girl children came to sit under my branches with a young man I had not seen before. They were sitting very close together with arms intertwined. The man took out a small knife and began to cut into my bark. It did hurt me a little, but I figured he wouldn't be able to do too much damage with such a small knife. What he did was to carve a heart and put his name and the girl's name inside that heart. I decided it was pretty cool to share their love for each other.

Many years have gone by. All the children went away. I noticed Steve and Ann didn't get around much anymore. Their hair turned white and they spent a lot more time sitting in their chairs under my branches. Then one day I didn't see them anymore, they were gone. I wondered what would happen to me and the house they lived in, we were feeling awfully lonely.

But I didn't have to worry because one day I saw that same young man, and the girl who had carved their names in my trunk, move into the house. I am sure they are going to have babies of their own. I can hardly wait until their little ones climb into my arms again and fill my life with joy.

MONKEY BUSINESS

I was watching a program on TV the other evening. It was about scientists who are discovering how intelligent monkeys are. They have known for some time that the larger apes such as orangutans, gorillas and chimpanzees are capable of reasoning and using tools. They are now discovering that monkeys also are very clever.

For instance, there are a few towns in Thailand where monkeys have become integrated into the city life, so much so that the people have festivals where they put out great quantities of fruit on the streets just for the monkeys. After the feast is over, the monkeys jump up on the shoulders of the women with long hair. They then pluck out a few hairs, run away to use the hair as dental floss and clean their teeth of food scraps.

In a monkey sanctuary in central Africa, there is a large monkey that has been raised with humans; his name is "Conley". He understands English language perfectly but, of course, can't speak. His trainers have devised picture symbols where he can point out his thoughts for communication. There are over five hundred symbols that he uses regularly.

His trainers told him they were going on a picnic and what would he like to take in his rucksack. He picked out four or five fruits and marshmallows. After eating the fruit, Conley piled a few twigs on the ground. He then took a box of matches, took out a match and lit it on the side of the box, then held the lighted match to the twigs to start a small fire. His next step was to line up some marshmallows on a stick and hold them over the fire to brown. He proceeded to eat them with great relish. After his little treat, he got a small bottle of water, took a drink and then poured the remainder of the water on the fire to put it out. Of course, obviously he had learned to copy this whole sequence but it was still a remarkable feat. He is getting old and is now teaching his young son all he knows.

As a child growing up in India, there were numerous times when we interacted with monkeys. It was not uncommon for a band of monkeys to descend on a well cultivated garden full of flowers and in a few short minutes devour every blossom in sight.

But our closet contact came when we travelled by train. There were no dining cars so everyone packed their own food or purchased something to eat from food vendors at the train stations. At many of the stops monkeys had learned to take advantage of this. The trains had no sealed windows and the open windows were a way to let in fresh air. The troops of monkeys also discovered it was an excellent way to steal a meal. They would run along the roof of the train as it stopped at a station, find an open window and jump right into the compartment to snatch away food sitting around and scamper away back out the window. We learned to close windows or to hang on to our food for dear life.

No one seemed to be upset by these monkey robbers. We just all learned to adapt to their tricks, it was just part of the fun of life in India.

It is interesting to discover that our animal friends are smarter and more adaptable than we thought they were. Perhaps we humans are not the only species to learn from experience.

WHAT HAPPENED TO OUR TAIL?

I am pretty sure they are right about this evolution thing. It seems quite clear that we humans climbed up the tree of evolution to be the most advanced and smartest of all the primates. After all, our DNA is more than 97% the same as chimpanzees and such. But I have one serious question: why did we lose our tails? Oh, I can hear you now; you're saying "good riddance". Think of all the problems we would have if we had to worry about a tail. Our clothes would not fit. Perhaps we would have to have an extra pant leg to hold our tails. If they just hung out there in the open they would be a real bother getting caught in elevators, car doors, etc. Besides all that, even our chairs and sofas would have to have a special hole for our tails.

So, you ask, why in the world would we want tails? I can think of several advantages that having a tail would accomplish. First of all, there is the matter of balance. Think how cool it would be if you wanted to walk a tightrope, instead of a balance pole your tail could do that job. Then, think about how useful tails are to express our emotions, our dog and cat friends can show us, in an instant, about how they are feeling. We could wag our tails with joy, switch our tails when angry, tuck them between our legs when we are afraid and raise them straight up in the air to show confidence. That way, other people would get our message, even across the room, we wouldn't need to say a thing! Then consider when we go swimming? If we had a tail we could flip it back and forth behind us to help us swim faster. It might even work as a rudder to help steer us in the right direction; and how about when we are caught outside on a hot day. We could hold our tails over our heads to make some shade. Or even flip them back and forth to work like a fan and cool us. There is one more thing I think tails would be good for. When you are trying to sleep and it is cold, we could just use our tails to curl around us to keep toasty warm.

Of course, this whole idea really doesn't matter a whit: we are as we are. Our tails just got left behind a long time ago. But it does make me wonder why. In one way, it would be kind of fun if we all still had tails.

WHO IS IN CHARGE?

This essay is not written for anyone born in the "Computer Generation"; only those of us who grew up in a simpler time will relate to my situation. To be honest with you, I was secretly relieved to be retiring from teaching in 1988 just as the whole school system was changing over to computers. I rather liked the simple process of doing grades, etc. by hand.

But not all aspects of life can avoid the change to a digital world. My husband, Fred, and I bought a lovely new Lexus in 2007. It had all the "bells and whistles" possible. The seats could be preprogrammed to adjust to each individual driver. There were separate climate controls for every occupant; the marvels went on and on. We spent many hours studying the owner's manual until it became dog-eared with use. It seemed hard to remember all the necessary steps to achieve a desired result.

However, there were a few things the car did on its own. We found out we were unable to change some of its ways. For instance: if any moisture touched the windshield the wipers would automatically start swiping back and forth. On occasion, we would return to our carefully locked car to find the windows open. We suspected the car didn't like to get too hot inside the passenger compartment.

I remembered it was a bit like my experiences with riding a horse. Not feeling too confident, I always knew I was not the one in charge. The horse went along with the game, but still had the upper hand whenever he wanted it.

So, we decided to name our new car "Hal", alter the computer's name in the movie "2001: A Space Odyssey." In that movie the computer began to gain unwanted control of the space mission. When the operator sad to the computer "I am going to shut you down" the computer replied in an ominous low voice, "I don't think so. I am in charge now!"

So it was. Our car, Hal, cooperated with us most of the time. But we always felt a little intimidated for we *all knew* who was really in charge.

I understand the cars of the future will take over completely. They can be programmed to even do the driving, avoiding collisions, slowing and stopping when desired. The driver and passengers can sleep or read a book or whatever. Perhaps those cars of the future will even decide where they want to go! That is when computers will really be in charge. They will only need people around to keep them in good running order.

THE MIRACLE OF LIFE

At this stage of my life I have a lot of time to just sit around and think. In my one good ear, that still works, I can hear my pulse switching through my head. Not loud enough to be a constant distraction, but nevertheless, always there. This has gotten me to thinking about my heart. Throughout my entire life I have taken my body's processes for granted. Now, in the face of possible failure, I realize how very important all these functions are; I think I have grown to appreciate my heart most of all.

In fact, I feel almost sentimental about my faithful, ever hardworking heart. It was the very first organ to get it all started. Within a few short days after conception that tiny little heart started to beat. From that moment to this day, some eighty plus years later, it has faithfully kept on beating. What an amazing accomplishment.

From these thoughts my mind turns to the miracle of birth. Just the idea of how the complex form of a human grows from a tiny speck of matter is truly a miracle. All this happens in the span of nine months. I remember the time of my two children's births, during pregnancy I knew a baby was developing but to actually see a perfect little human appear, was one of the most profound experiences of my life.

This same sense of wonder can touch us as we observe the world around us. Even the wonder of how a flower, or tree, can grow from just a little seed.

Most of our pets were neutered, so we didn't observe the process of birth very often, but on one occasion, Fred my husband, and I did share a very special little drama of birth.

Our retirement home in Tucson was on a golf course. It was a joy to watch the variety of wildlife attracted to this lush environment. One of our favorites were the families of plump little desert quails as they foraged through the grasses and shrubbery. In the lead was daddy quail with his bobbing topknot followed closely by a line of babies, sometimes as many as eight of them. Then, at the rear, was mama quail making sure none of the babies got lost.

One spring, during mating season, we noticed a quail couple checking out our patio tor a potential nesting site. They decided on a large potted azalea palm right outside our large picture window. It was a large pot, which was some two feet off the ground, with a tall bushy plant to offer concealment but there were a couple of problems with their choice our little dog, fritz, was quite attracted to the presence of the birds and kept standing on his back legs to check out the nest. We placed the pot up on the top of a small table so fritz couldn't reach it. The other problem was watering: as the eggs started to appear, I decided the little quail family had the first priority; I could always buy another plant.

So the little drama began to unfold before us, we could watch it all from behind the glass window without disturbing the birds. They didn't build a nest, only hollowed out a small depression in the mulch in the pot. Then the female bird began to lay one egg each day, each about the size of a marble. But much to our surprise she didn't stay to sit on them. Finally, after laying nine eggs, she settled down to brood. That meant uncompromising devotion, after hours on the nest she would leave only if the male was there to take over the job while she went off to feed.

After about twenty one days, the day of hatching finally arrived and both mom and dad were in close attention. From each tiny little egg there emerged a little bird not much larger than a miniature marshmallow. Soon, as the feathers dried, they turned into tiny balls of fluff. Within a few hours all but one of the eggs had hatched. Soon the flowerpot seemed to be full of tiny chicks dashing around on the soil under the plant.

We became concerned when we noticed the parents were not bringing any food to the nest, in fact, they seemed to spend a lot of time away. But we discovered they had another plan. On the third day after hatching we heard a lot of loud quail calling from the patio beside the flowerpot. Both dad and mom were there calling to the babies. I became really concerned, how would those tiny little puff balls, with hardly any wings, be able to leave the pot, which stood at least three to four feet off the ground without hurting themselves. I soon saw I had no reason for concern; one by one the little chicks jumped up on the edge of the pot and flung themselves out into midair, so light and fluffy they almost floated to the ground. Mom and dad kept up their vocal encouragement, even though several of the chicks seemed to be a bit reluctant to launch themselves off into space.

One interesting observation was the parents seemed to know when all the babies had joined them. They never flew up to the nest to check, but when the eighth chick jumped down they all gathered together and off they went around the side of the house dad in the lead, all eight tiny chicks following in a line, with mom bringing up the rear: they never came back. We wished them a safe and successful lifetime of adventure, and for us, a rare glimpse into another miracle of life.

OLD AGE FROM A CHILD'S POINT OF VIEW

For the young child the prospect of growing old someday has no relevance. Their thoughts are focused on what is occurring in the present, perhaps with some plans for what might happen when they grow up. Even the idea that one will grow old and feeble is hardly worth considering.

As a high school teacher, one of my student's common questions was "How old are you"? Being in my forties I thought that saying I was 93 would get a response of disbelief. However, much to my chagrin, the response was more often "oh, then you must have been teaching for a long time".

A friend told me of a conversation with her young grandson. He was looking at her sagging skin and remarked "grandma, it looks like you're melting".

This all brings me to my memory of a teacher at my boarding School, Edith Jones. The story was that she had been an Elementary teacher from the early years of the school. She had never married and her years there were her whole life of dedication. After retiring from teaching she was given the right to continue living in her apartment.

From our point of view, as inexperienced pre-teenagers, we considered her to be "ancient". She was probably in her seventies, but with white hair, stooped over posture and lots of wrinkles, we imagined she was at least a hundred years old.

As a pre-teenager I recall that she was our "blue bird" leader (a junior phase of girl scouts). We actually didn't do much except line up, Do a few marching patterns and win badges for handicrafts. I imagine she was really not up to any serious campouts, etc.

However, my most vivid memory of our dear Edith Jones was during my high school years. The school medical facilities, and hospital where students were admitted for minor ailments was close to her apartment. She was a sweet and loving person and wanted to make our stay in the hospital as positive as possible. This included her idea that she would make the rounds to each occupant to bestow on each one a goodnight kiss, regardless of age or gender. This really was the last thing any of us wanted. Dear Miss Jones not only had bad breath but also an extensive crop of stiff, wiry whiskers and mustache. Any new patients were told by those already there of this hazard. The only way to escape the kisses was by pretending to already be asleep. So upon hearing her approach, everyone would immediately roll over with eyes closed, pretending to be asleep, hoping this would work to tend off her attentions. Of course, looking back to that time, it was insensitive of us to act in that way.

Now that I am the same age as our dear Miss Jones was, I wonder how I am perceived by the young; probably with some mild curiosity and interest in what old age does to one. But, given time, they too will reach old age and be able to look back at the attitudes they had when they were young.

GENERATIONAL "CRUSHES"

The other day I was watching a women's talk show on TV. It seems that for these women George Clooney is the "current hottie", the newest term for what we used to call "having a crush"on someone of the opposite sex.

Way, way back, when I was in high school, the object of my group of girl friends was Gary Cooper. That self assured, manly mystique had all our hearts aflutter. Somehow I had procured a larger than life size poster of my crush; he was looking directly into my eyes with a look of total seduction. I kidded with my friends that having that picture on my bedroom wall made me self conscious undressing with him watching me that way!

Of course men have crushes too. All the famous pin-up pictures during WWII of Betty Grable and Rita Hayworth were well publicized. My boyfriend during high school had a crush on Teresa Wright. I remember wondering what I could do to make me look more like her. Elizabeth Taylor and Ava Gardner have also made many a male's heart beat faster.

In the years since that high school crush on Gary Cooper, I have had a few more: Robert Redford in the movie "downhill racer" was one. I never fell for the "pretty boys" like Tyrone power or Paul Newman. During my years of teaching the heart throb of most of the women on the staff was Tom Seleck. His rugged good looks turned us all into piles of mush. And I have a confession to make, even to this day, although he is now well past his virile prime, he still is my "hottie". If I had a poster of him in my bedroom I would still feel a little shy.

On the other hand, maybe I will try to find a new one; it might just spark up my routine.

MAYBE PART MONKEY?

I don't remember when it all began, but as far back as I can recall I loved to climb trees. I am sure my brother, Stan, must have had something to do about it. He did like to get me involved in all sorts of adventures and challenges. I do remember that one time when he was about seven or eight years old he climbed up into a large sycamore tree that grew in our backyard. His objective was to steal the eggs from a hawk's nest high up in the tree. He succeeded in reaching the nest even with constant attacks from the angry mother bird. But it seemed that his short pants pockets were not the ideal place to carry the eggs, for as he attempted to make a rather desperate retreat down the tree the eggs were all smashed. The look on his face as he walked towards the house with rotten egg slime dripping down his legs was never to be forgotten. He had to endure lots of teasing from our family.

Perhaps one reason I loved to climb trees is because there were so many good trees to climb. On the plains of India grew the massive banyan trees with low hanging horizontal branches. A perfect place to crawl out onto the bouncy tips where one could swing up and down. It was also easy to climb up high into the upper branches where numerous crooks and crannies could be found.

The trees that grew in the Himalayan Mountains, where we went to school, were also great for climbing. The oak trees were huge with broad branches covered by soft green moss. I discovered many cozy little nooks high up in the trees to spend time dreaming, or even reading a book.

The tall pine trees were a bit of a challenge. It was difficult to reach the lowest branches, but when you did it was easy to climb on up to the very top of the pine tree where you could sway back and forth in the wind. The one other problem with pine trees was the sticky sap that got all over your hands and clothes. Not something mother liked to see.

My friends and I spent many happy hours up in trees with games of Tarzan or imaginary ships sailing across the ocean, or perhaps the tree was a house of many rooms to explore!

This love for climbing trees persisted into adulthood. On our family camping trips I introduced our two sons to the joy of climbing. However, I did notice that somehow it wasn't quite as easy as it was when I was a child.

The last time I recall climbing a tree was when I was in my late thirties. We were visiting my brother John's family back in New Jersey for Christmas. I offered to make a table decoration. I saw some interesting large seed pods hanging on one of the bare trees in the yard, so thinking they would add to the decoration, with some nice gold spray, I clambered up into the tree. Whereupon an agitated neighbor called my brother on the phone to advise him of observing a woman up in one of his trees. My brother reassured him that it was all OK, that the woman was just his crazy sister.

Of course, many years have passed since my tree climbing days. At this age, it is enough to manage climbing a flight of stairs. But still, whenever I see a large branched tree, I am apt to look it over for the best route to take to climb up into its inviting arms. After all, deep inside I am perhaps still part monkey!

IN THE NAME OF RELIGION

Since the beginning of the Homo sapiens when we were hunter-gathers man has been searching for a way to control our destinies. For early man, with his close connection with nature, he looked for ways to influence the sun and rain with ceremonies and dances. Even in today's world there are societies that live so close to nature they still look to a more powerful deity to provide for rain and sun to bring them prosperity. The American Indian culture of the fourteen hundreds, and even today thank the animal or fish they have killed to be a sacrifice for their wellbeing.

As our societies became more complex, we discovered that to get along with each other we needed to show tolerance and love to oil the wheels of society. The renegades, who could not follow the rules, would have to be ostracized or punished.

In the search for the meaning of life and death, we humans established religions to give us the answers. Throughout time from the very simplest worship of nature to highly organized and ritualistic practices, we have looked to a deity for the meaning of our existence.

Some of these religions have been tolerant to others who don't believe as they do. The Hindu religion of India is an example; they have hundreds of gods. You can worship any god you want. Included in their gods are Mohamed and Jesus. Other religions such as Christianity and Muslim beliefs have had a past history of intolerance. During the crusades when the crusaders stormed out of England to kill Jews and Muslims. Then during the rule of Queen Elizabeth the first Protestants and Catholics in France and England were killing each other. Even in our time, the hatred of Protestants and Catholics in Ireland led to years of warfare.

In the years following the establishment of the Muslim faith, as the new religion swept through North Africa, the zealots killed anyone not willing to accept the new faith. But by the time they reached Spain they became more tolerant. There was a golden era in Spain where Muslims, Jews and Christians lived in harmony. As a child growing up in India there was a tolerance for all religions; Hindus, Muslims and Christians lived in harmony side by side. It was only with the independence of India from British rule in 1947 that the trouble began. The majority of the populations were Hindus; Jinna was the leader of the Muslim population. He was fearful that the Muslims would not have a voice in the new democratic government. He demanded that the provinces be divided into two nations by the determination of which provinces had a majority of Muslims or Hindus. So was created the nations of Pakistan and India.

That is when the turmoil began. With families feeling uncomfortable in an environment of being a minority, both Muslims and Hindus wanted to make a move. That is when intolerance showed its ugly head. The killing began. The city of Calcutta was evenly divided between Muslims, and Hindus. One terrible day they clashed on one of the bridges, hundreds of people were massacred and thrown off the bridge into the river below. On the trains, which passed from India into Pakistan the families, hoping to relocate, were slaughtered as they passed into hostile country. Even today, some seventy years later, there is still bad blood between the two nations.

In the present time we have the growing threat of Isis, a radical branch of the Muslim faith. It is so important not to paint all Muslims with the same brush. The great majority are peace loving and tolerant.

Down through the centuries mankind has fought over religion. What a better world we would have if only we could be more understanding and tolerant of others beliefs and religious faiths.

THE BEST OF TIMES

Having the good fortune to still be alive after eighty years, I have been able to observe many transitions in our way of life. For example, from the Model T to the present day luxury of the electric car. From silent movies to epics of spectacular grandeur, and even the reality of 3D viewing. From phoning an operator to place a call to cell phones with all their tantalizing applications. From overseas travel by ship, taking weeks to get to far-off foreign lands to air travel taking less than eighteen hours to reach the most distant destinations. The only reason to take a cruise today is just the fun of the cruise life. From keeping in touch with family or friends by letter to instant communication by email or texting. From preparing meals "from scratch" then to frozen dinners now; to just dropping by any market to pick up dinner already prepared from the deli counter. From sitting around a radio to watching a wide variety of programs on massive TV sets with remote controls.

It is all truly amazing to consider what the advancement of technology has done to change our everyday experiences. Of course these changes have made our lives much easier. But have we lost something very precious along the way? I would like to suggest that we have. As I see it, the midyears of the twentieth century were the best era for those of us fortunate enough to live in America. Now, I know just what you are thinking! Every generation of elders says the same thing, "Our lives were so much better when we were young, etc., etc." But hear me out. I will try to explain why this is true. In the late 1940s we came out of WWII as the dominant and most prosperous nation in the world. We had won two wars fought on opposite sides of the world. We were not only full of national pride, but we also saw the future with glowing optimism. The economy was booming. Anyone who wanted to work could find a job. Women were liberated from being "stay at home moms" or nursing or teaching. All fields were now open to her, if she so desired.

The mass production of household appliances made life easier and left time to engage in leisure activities. With the higher standard of living, but with prices still low, families were able to buy homes and cars, with enough left over to do some worldwide traveling. And when you traveled to the exotic places they still retained their unique ways of costumes, food, culture, music and language. Unlike today with a homogenous blending of clothing, food and speech. There seems to be a McDonalds in every far-out place. To travel overseas was an interesting adventure. But now with mass media and worldwide marketing it will be hard to find any place where you can find a unique way of life.

But the most precious thing we seem to be losing is much harder to explain. There seems to be a loss of connection between family and friends. Young adults brag about having thousands of "friends" on Facebook, but what does that really mean? Do you really know those friends? With instant texting and compacted messages do you really know how they are facing up to life's challenges? As a child and also with my children, evenings and weekends were spent making up games like "kick the can" and baseball with the neighborhood kids. We learned the give and take of life, and how to best get along. Today's children are all into organized sports with no chance to develop life skills. It is great to be in constant touch with family and friends, but what happened to the friendly chat on the phone where you discussed your worries and problems? Also I do concede it is a marvel to have any information you might need to know at your fingertips on the internet. It surely beats going to a dictionary or library.

Somehow we seem to be losing the ability to make close connections. There is a self-centeredness and preoccupation with gadgets that are replacing the close bonds we once had with those around us. Perhaps it is just the ramblings of an old lady, but I do think we have lost something very precious when we latched on to all the conveniences of the world today. Three cheers for the good old days!!

CIRCLES OF LOVE

It seems that the capacity to love does not happen spontaneously. It is an emotion that is nurtured by receiving love and a sense of security as an infant. Babies that are raised without being shown that they are loved are unable as adults to have the capacity to love another person.

I visualize a newborn child in the center of circles. His capacity for love can spread out in ever expanding circles. First is the love he feels for his mother who cares for his needs and shows him how to love. Next comes the family with siblings and lessons in sharing and caring. The next circle includes playmates and other adults outside the family. On reaching adulthood the fortunate ones find a partner to marry and share a lifetime of love and caring. With children coming along one has the wonderful opportunity to share how it is to love.

For many people this is as far as their capacity to love goes. But for a few their circle of love keeps growing, often to include the whole world. Healthcare volunteers, missionaries, teachers and disaster relief workers often risk their own lives to help others in need. The line is blurred between love and compassion. Most of us are touched with compassion when we hear of someone in tragic circumstances, but it takes that special person with a full capacity for love to reach beyond their comfort zone to show how much they can love.

— POEMS —

The Call of the Wild Geese

The trees outside my window are dressed in their finest gold

Gone are their cloaks of summer green

They stand there and wait for the cold winds of autumn to snatch away

Their lovely dresses

Leaving their branches naked and bare

The sun sparkles in a clear blue sky

A denial of the dark and gloomy days to come

From high above the trees I hear the call of wild geese

I look up to see the wedge of birds on their southern flight

Their haunting call invites me to fly away with them

To far-off lands of adventure and intrigue

Alas, I have no wings to soar with them in giddy flight

But in my heart I dream of the journey soaring high above

To warm and gentle places where the cold winds of winter never come

Snowfall

Soft, white snowflakes drift down by my window

No hint of breeze to push them away

They float quietly down, one by one, to meet the dark, warm earth below

There, the first to fall melt away and are gone

But with each melting flake the dark earth begins to cool

Soon, for those who follow, find a place to rest on one another

As I watch, the soft fluff of snow is cradled on every branch and bush

The cooled earth welcomes its soft white blanket

The magic of the fluffy snow turns the whole world outside my window

To fairyland of white

The clouds move on

The flakes no longer fall

The sun looks down to turn the whole scene to sparkling diamonds

The garden sleeps and dreams of the spring to come, under its soft, light
blanket of white

My Box of Treasures

I only have to lift the lid of memories

To find the treasures deep within.

The jewels that rest there sparkle and gleam.

They fill me with joy and delight.

Those memories rest in layers of time.

Beneath them all, the childhood days.

Each passing year new layers form

To cover over the fading past.

I reach deep down to find hidden gems

To remember the times of long ago.

But I must use care in my probing search

For some of those memories have sharp edges

That can cut and slash my heart with pain.

'Tis best to put those ones aside.

My treasure box is my constant companion

But the years have begun to take their toll.

With cracks and holes on every side

Where precious memories slip away.

Each time I look the gems are fewer.

Too soon, to find they all have gone.

But for this time the joy lives on

Sweet memories to find and share.

My treasure box of sparkling gems

To hold and cherish for this brief time.

On Silver Wings

All passengers to comply.

Electronics turned off

Seat belts secured

Seats to the upright

All baggage stowed.

Our bird of shining silver,

And outstretched wings

With utmost care

Moves slowly past others

Still at rest in their stalls.

She takes her place

At the runway's end

Pauses a moment, then

With a mighty roar of power

Hurtles down the track

Every fiber straining

to break free of gravity's pull

Against all logic, suddenly

The heavy, monstrous bird

Has lifted free

From the clinging arms of Mother Earth.

With a shudder of delight

She soars on her way

To the skies above.

Frequent travelers pay no heed

They read their books

Or rest with eyes closed.

But I, seated by my window,

Delight in the magic of it all.

Dusk has fallen--dark clouds all about

We are soon inside their dusky core.

But then we break free

The gray clouds become a floor below.

There, above us, I see

Yet another layer of clouds.

They are not dark and gray

But of soft, fluffy white.

We are floating in the space between.

Our bird is still climbing

We pass through those billows of white

At last we are free

To soar in a sky of azure blue.

In the west, the sun is setting

Below us, each towering white cloud

Is touched with shimmering gold.

What a glorious sight to behold

We fly away into the night

To find a sky full of stars

And then, a full moon

To top off the show.

Soft moonlight shimmers

On our bird's silver wings.

This mighty bird is taking me home.

To walk, once more, with my feet on the ground

But for this brief time

I have broken those bonds
I have flown high above.
To dance with the stars
I have soared like a bird
In a magical flight.

Saddlebrooke—
A Place My Soul Calls Home

There is a place of clear blue skies

Where saguaros stand proud and tall,

Where open vistas fill your gaze

Where stars, alone, can light the night with

All their brilliance and profusion.

A desert place of rolling hills

Pressed close to towering mountain peaks,

Where pine trees grow and wild cougars roam,

This is a place my soul calls home.

The hand of man has done his share

With hills of green and sparkling ponds,

A haven for creatures of the wild

To make their homes and flourish there.

The cautious rabbits and gentle deer,

The javelina with their destructive ways,

The wily coyote looking for a meal,

The comic roadrunner and beloved quail

Who herd their chicks with watchful care.

So many other birds with joyful song

To fill the air with vibrant life,

All this an oasis where nature thrives

In delicate balance to benefit all.

But lest you think tranquility rules,

There is another violent face when

Summer rains transform the place.

The morning brings no hint of what will come

For by noon dark thunderclouds appear
And soon the wondrous show begins
With rolling thunder and lightning flashes
Then a deluge of rain to match Niagara
To make rivers of water in every place.
You think Noah's ark might save the day.
But then, suddenly, the storm is past,
The sun reappears on a world refreshed.
The cooler air brings back songs of birds
The pulse of life returns again.
Though my life is far from this golden place,
In my dreams I live there still
To revel in clear desert air
To hear the song of the coyote's call
In the quiet moon-filled night
To sit alone in a peaceful place
And greet the rising sun
To spend my days in nature's arms
This is a place my soul calls home.

Pink Petal Dancers

Each little pink petal is part of the glory

A profusion of blossoms to welcome the spring

They wait impatiently, in their tree mother's arms

For the wind, their dance master, to set them free

To fly away in the sparkling air

To flutter and spin on their way to the ground

To gather with the millions already there

To join in the dance of the wind master's song

Each little pink petal is part of the show

With thousands of others they flutter and flow

With skirts held high they tiptoe and whirl

Like waves in the ocean they tumble and curl

What joy to be part of this glorious dance

With the wind as a teacher the ballet plays on

'Til tired and weary, the dancers need rest

They pile up together in soft pillows of pink

Like the white snowflake dancers of winters past

They wait for the wind to lift them again

To dance, one more time, to the music of spring

Nature's Cathedral

There is this hidden place where natures own cathedral stands

Mid towering sandstone cliffs of red and gold

It is a place where the master sculptors of water and wind, have down

Through countless ages, carved their masterpiece of curving stone

There, the light is soft and cool

There, the searching sun can find only the highest canyon walls to

Spread a golden glow on all that is below

This is a place of gentle sounds

The music of the stream as it tumbles over stone, still the sculptor at its

Endless task, carving ever deeper

The sweet haunting song of the canyon wren from a ledge in the cliffs

High above

But this is not a barren place for in this cathedral nature has added more

Along the stream the air is cool; pine and maple fill their spaces leaving

Room for gentle flowers to add color and perfume

An untouched garden of wild profusion

This is a place of deep connection

To find one's role in all creation

To feel the unhurried passage of endless time

To leave, for a while, the stresses of daily life

To know, they too will wash away

To understand that here, in this magic place

All is well and here is the place of peace

Where Has He Gone

It seems that just the other day he was here.

This one who shared my life.

The one who shared my jokes and fun.

The one who shared my problems, too,

Who could make it not seem so bad.

The one who made each adventure a delight,

Just because it was one we shared.

The one whose arms around me

Could make all else just fade away.

The One whose tender love and caring

Was the wind beneath my wings?

Where has He gone?

Here He sits close by my side.

His face familiar in every line.

His body stills the one beloved

But from those eyes the life has gone.

Instead the look of one who is lost.

For him life is all a forgotten dream.

What cruel fate has done this thing'?

To snatch away his very essence

To leave only an empty shell

To carry on

I wish I knew where he has gone!

How Can I Say Goodbye?

How can I say goodbye
To the one who shared my journey
And walked with me, hand in hand
On the path of life
So many miles through fields of flowers
To fill our lives with love and joy
To find our way through quiet forests
Where we could rest in tranquil peace
To come across a sparkling stream
That filled our hearts with fun and laughter
To find a few boulders in the way
That took our love and caring to move aside
To climb the heights of a mountain peak
While embraced in the passion of loving arms
And now l turn for a loving touch
To find that he is gone
He left, without me, on around the bend
Out of sight, but not forgotten
For he left with me so many memories
To comfort and sustain me
With those sweet memories l can carry on
To travel the path alone
There is no need to say goodbye,
For l know he waits for me
On ahead beyond that future bend
So we can be together for all time

Growing Old is Not So Bad

Growing old is not so bad

It has its compensations

You no longer have to assert yourself

In numerous situations

The clothes you have will do just fine

No need to stay with fashion

For comfort is your final goal

To heck with frivolous passions

Wrinkles tell of years gone by

They show where you have been

With sight turned dim and details gone

It helps when you can't see them

Then comes along the loss of hearing

But sometimes that is not so bad

The modern music and filthy slang

To tune it out can make you glad

With aching joints and body pain

No need to wake at dawn

To run for miles and drive ourselves

To practice for the marathon

Then when our hair turns white

Others show deference

By opening doors and helping us

We can enjoy a sense of preference

So fellow oldies take soon cheer

Our lives are not all bad

After all we are still here

For which we should be.